THE LEGEND OF
FIREBALL FLEMING

The Legend of
Fireball Fleming

Pete Gagan

To order additional copies of this book, contact:
Xlibris Corporation
1-888-795-4274
www.Xlibris.com
Orders@Xlibris.com
39479

Contents

FOREWORD

The "Legend of Fireball Fleming" is a historical novel set during the pioneer days of motorcycling in America. The story begins with Jed Fleming's presence at the early experiments of Sylvester Roper and the colorful Edward Joel Pennington, and continues through the board track racing era to the early twenties, and finishes with the stock market crash of 1929 which ends Jed's career. That exciting period saw the invention of the motorcycle, and its development from crude powered bicycles to 100 plus mile an hour overhead camshaft, and four valve headed racing machines, and sophisticated road bikes like Indian's Hendee Special, with electric lighting, electric starter, and swing arm rear suspension. As you follow this period, you will realize that most major developments were made during that era, and very little else is new.

Jed "Fireball" Fleming, his family, and a few of his friends are fictional characters. The motorcycle personalities he meets during his motorcycling career are real people, and most of the events and activities he participates in are historical. I have taken some literary license in re-creating some of these events for reasons of entertainment, but have tried to remain true to history. Unfortunately, the recorded motorcycle history I've referred to is not always accurate, so I apologize for any shortcomings. This lack of accuracy is due in large to the fact that at the time these events took place, journalism was inaccurate and subject to exaggeration, as it often is today. I've used parts of George Wyman's story as he wrote it in The Motorcycle Magazine in their November issue of 1903, as I could not improve on his writings.

Fireball himself is somewhat of a wastrel and scoundrel. Had he been otherwise, given the opportunities presented to him, he would have become a historical character. Being fictional he could not. I hope you enjoy his tale.

Pete Gagan, January, 2007

CHAPTER ONE

TACOMA, WASHINGTON, 1944

Jed Fleming was cold through to his bones. He felt it worse than most men of his age, as his body was riddled with arthritis, mostly due to the fact he'd broken most of those bones at one time or another during his youth. His mostly-gray hair still showed trace evidence of a youthful, fiery red. The climate of the Northwest was milder than other parts of the country he'd lived in all of his life, but it sure was damp, and he hadn't seen the sun in weeks. Years before, in the dirty thirties, Jed had hopped a westward-bound freight train. He had hoped to make a fortune cutting timber in the Pacific Northwest. When he got there, he probably would have starved to death if it hadn't been for the soup kitchens. "Thank God for the war," Jed would say. He finally took a job as a welder, building Liberty Ships in Tacoma's shipyards. It was tough sledding because of his arthritis; handling and lifting the steel plates was a painful challenge. And, because it was piecework, his pay packet was usually lighter than those of his co-workers.

According to the Betty Grable Calendar on the wall, it was February 29th, his *fifteenth* birthday. Having a birthday only once every four years, usually made them special. "Not this one," thought Jed. While he was just sixty, actually, he felt more like eighty—a lonely old guy living in a crappy part of town, freezing his ass off. He decided he'd better get off his butt and gather some firewood to warm the place up some.

Jed picked up his crow bar and Swede saw, and headed outside to his trusty Model A pickup, which, like everything else outside, was wet. Moss grew on the boards of the truck's box. It was old and rusty, and he was still making payments on it. Behind the wheel, he turned the gas tap on, pulled out the choke rod, twisting it counter clockwise to enrich the mixture and, after retarding the spark lever, pushed the floor-mounted starter knob with his foot. With its tinny exhaust sound, the old truck leapt to life.

Always the good mechanic, Jed let it run for a few minutes with the spark retarded and the manifold heater open. The exhaust manifold on a Model A will soon glow a cherry red when the ignition is retarded, so the manifold heater warmed the cab quickly. "I'm sure glad I winterized the old girl," he said to no one in particular. Unable to afford antifreeze, Jed ran used crankcase oil in the radiator during the winter months. The old Ford was a very tolerant piece of equipment. Jed put the truck in gear and headed towards the best supply of free firewood in the northwest, the old Tacoma Board Track, built in 1912, but left to rot after closing in 1922.

As the Ford rattled along the potholed surface of Highway 99, Jed grumbled to himself about the lousy maintenance on the roads, one of the more unpleasant effects of the war. He scanned the gas gauge on the dashboard: he could hear the cork float tapping the bottom of the tank. The needle was showing near empty: by Jed's reckoning, just enough to get home. The damned gas was almost twenty cents a gallon when you were lucky enough to get any. He soon got to the site, about 3 miles south of town, just off the highway.

At the remains of the old track, Jed noticed other scroungers gathering boards and planks for firewood, as well as for various construction projects. There was very little evidence of the handsome, original track. It had been two miles in length, oval in shape, and banked on the ends. It had been wide enough for several cars to run abreast, or a half-dozen sidecar outfits. Built in 1912, it had thrilled crowds with racing until 1922, when it had been shut down. Racing had become increasingly dangerous as the wood rotted—particularly on the banked ends. The stands had long disappeared, as well as the banked corners. The two straight-aways had survived, as they were used as runways for Tacoma's first Municipal airport. That in turn had been abandoned before the war. Stacks of lumber survived though, as did some of the surface. The 2x6s and 2x8s were laid on edge to form the wooden racing surface, providing a good deal of useable lumber in what remained of the old track.

Jed went to work with his crowbar prying boards apart and removing nails. The Swede saw quickly sliced the boards into suitable lengths. He secured his load, and got the hell out of there. Theoretically, he was stealing the wood, as were the others; but what good was it to anybody? The cops came and harassed people anyway. It had always been like that, reflected Jed.

Due to the oil spilled from monster race cars like Ralph De Palma's Duesenberg, and the ported, brakeless, racing motorcycles that used to thrill crowds, some of the boards were in pretty good shape and free of rot. Jed had picked his lumber well. Back home he soon had a great fire going in his big, old pot-bellied stove that he'd found at the dump.

Jed sat in his comfortable, old chair, gazing at the flames through the mica window of the stove door as his body welcomed the satisfying heat. Jed noticed the blue smoke coming from the oil-soaked wood, some it escaping through the cracked lid of the stove. The scent of the burning oil aroused memories of exciting machinery and engines roaring at high speeds. A parade of vague, long-ago faces appeared in the smoky window: a sketchy roll call of those he had spent his life with—worked with, laughed with, argued with . . . and would remain with him always.

CHAPTER TWO

WISCONSIN, 1896

Jed was born on a farm near Racine Wisconsin on Feb 29th, 1884, to Zeke and Hanna Fleming with distinctive, flaming red hair. It was a tough birth. Hanna would often say later, "After the good Lord brought us Jedidiah, He decided that we would have no more children." She always felt that Jed, a leap-year baby, was born for some great cause, as the Lord also gave him that special birthday. Although she never complained, Jed would always sense a note of disappointment in her voice whenever his mother expressed this sentiment. Jed was less than impressed by the February 29th birthday than his mother, as other kids had a birthday every year. As an only child though, Jed enjoyed the fact that his parents always made a very big deal out of his infrequent birthdays.

Jed thought back to his third birthday, when he received a Star bicycle. He could hardly wait for the winter snows to melt, so he could ride it. The 1890's were the era of the bicycle, when over 1200 manufacturers of bicycles thrived in the USA alone. The *Pony Star*, manufactured in Smithville, New Jersey, was second hand—a "high wheeler," or "ordinary," as they were known. This was a type that was fast disappearing in favor of the new-fangled "safety" bicycles. Safety bicycles had equal-sized wheels, fitted with a chain or shaft drive.

Jed's *Pony Star* had a slightly smaller drive wheel than most high wheelers though, including earlier Stars. It sported a drive system with straps and ratchets, making the huge drive wheel unnecessary. The four-foot diameter wheel made handling slightly easier than the five to six-foot monsters found in most ordinaries. On Jed's model the large wheel was on the rear rather than the front, typical of most ordinaries: the manufacturer described it as a "high-wheeled safety." The idea was to prevent the dangerous forward falls that plagued the riders of these tall bicycles. Nevertheless, it made the Star a difficult machine to master; backward falls could be almost as harmful as forward falls. These shortcomings were not a problem for 12 year-old Jed though: he was tall for his age, and used to hard work on the farm, was quite strong. Also blessed with exceptional physical co-ordination, Jed soon became an accomplished *wheelman* and, proudly, the youngest member of the local bicycle club. He rode his bicycle into town on a regular basis to compete against other riders on the quarter-mile velodrome in Racine.

Primarily a dairy farm, the Fleming farm managed to grow few crops, mostly as feed for their prize Holsteins. Zeke Fleming was a moderately wealthy farmer; he had a hired hand as well as Jed for help. Jed's favorite farm activity involved the threshing, when the crew came with their big steam engine and thresher. The steam engine held a special fascination for Jed: he would stand nearby, giving it a studied look by the hour and pestering the operators with questions. He learned the terms for the various parts and had an early understanding of such things as pistons, rods, cross heads, boiler tubes and their related functions. Once, when returning from Racine on his bicycle, Jed spotted a threshing crew working on another farm. Jed stopped to check out the machine being used there. It wasn't a steamer, but a new type of machine, powered by an "internal combustion" engine. It was a noisy contraption mounted on a wagon.

The engine had just a small fuel tank, rather than a boiler, which, the operator explained, was coal oil—the same as used in the lamps at home. Jed asked more questions and learned more new terms. The hit-and-miss engine was the best thing he had ever seen. And, like most young boys, he thrilled to the explosions and the way the monstrous thing shook the ground when it ran. The threshing machine attached to it was full sized; yet the machine was far more compact than the horse drawn steam engines he'd seen previously. Jed pestered the operator for information, soaking up all he could learn about the hot-tube ignition, speed governor, and a starting process using gasoline. Jed eagerly looked forward to each issue of *Scientific American* to keep abreast of any new mechanical inventions.

One day while reading back issues of Scientific American, he came across an article that caused him a great deal of excitement. It was a ten-year-old issue featuring a Star bicycle, almost the same as his—fitted with a steam engine. The story described the work of Lucius Copeland, of Phoenix, Arizona, who developed the engine while working as an engineer in that city's flourmill. The engine was fitted to the front down-tube of the high-wheeled Star, and drove the big rear wheel utilizing a thin leather sewing machine belt. Copeland claimed the steam cycle was capable of 12 mph, and made traveling uphill as easy as down, running on lamp kerosene. A further advantage was that the engine could be detached from the bicycle, and used for various domestic chores, such as powering washing machines, and operating small equipment around the average farm or home. Jed saw an opportunity for some family politicking. He rushed home to tell his parents. However Zeke merely humored the boy by suggesting he do further research, believing that a radical invention ten years previous, something he had never heard of, was likely a mere pipe dream.

"Lucius Copeland and the Steam Star, 1884"

Returning to the library the following day, Jed found an ad in another publication that showed the bicycle, as well as three other steam vehicles, being marketed by the Northrop Manufacturing Company. Unbeknownst to our hero, he had discovered history's first commercial advertising for motor vehicles. Although the ad was old, Jed wrote to the Northrop Company, c/o the Star Bicycle Company in Smithville, New Jersey, asking about the steam bicycle and whether he could get an engine for his Pony Star. By return mail, Jed received a hand—written letter from Hezikiah Smith, the president of the Star organization. Mr. Smith thanked Jed for choosing a Star bicycle and sent information on the latest Star safeties—along with the suggestion that Jed could become a dealer in his area. All he had to do was buy a new bicycle, demonstrate it to friends, and his fortune would be made. As for the steam engine, the news was a disappointment. Mr. Copeland was no longer associated with the firm, and his engine had disappeared along with him. It was not very successful, apparently; the only steam vehicle left was a three-wheeled carriage that, according to Mr. Smith, was only useful after considerable modification by himself. He still used it to travel to and from his office in Smithville.

Buying a new bicycle was beyond Jed's means, and if he were in the market, he would be looking at one of the new chain drive, or "chainless," shaft-drive wheels, not another out-dated Star. Nevertheless, Jed continued to dream about cycling without pedaling.

Sitting on the front porch in July of 1895, surveying their little kingdom, Zeke and Hanna spotted a cloud of dust descending the hill in the direction of Racine. "Land sakes alive, he's going to kill himself on that bicycle!" exclaimed Hanna. "He always coasts down that hill as fast as he can."

As if on cue, they saw Jed emerge from the dust cloud without the bicycle, tumbling head over heels, the bicycle skidding on its side behind him. They both ran at top speed to find their son, lying in the ditch and groaning. "It's my shoulder!" exclaimed Jed, trying to control his tears. Zeke ran back to the farm and harnessed up the buckboard while Hanna comforted their son. Zeke placed Jed in the buckboard; slowly nudging his team of black Tennessee Walkers to give Jed a smooth ride home.

Doc Hanson arrived in a couple of hours, thanks to the new family telephone, and put Jed's arm in a sling. He had broken his collarbone—the first fracture in a lifetime of many.

Zeke was proud of his team of black horses. No other farmer in the area had anything like them. A couple of weeks after Jed's accident, Zeke decided to allow Jed to handle the prize team to deliver the day's milk supply to a Milwaukee hotel. Jed had never been allowed to handle the high strung team on his own, let alone to the big city, but Zeke decided he was ready. Together they loaded the milk cans on the buckboard. Soon Jed was on his way, watching Fred and Mollie's black behinds, their tails swaying in front of him.

Although Jed would never admit it to his pa, he would have been much happier on his bicycle. He was in total control on his bicycle; his crash was something he could have avoided if he had not allowed his attention to wander, as he thought about the mechanical mysteries of kerosene engines. Fred and Mollie, he knew, were unlike his bicycle: they had minds of their own, and could take matters into their own hands (or hooves). As the ten-mile trip progressed, Jed became a bit more relaxed, as Fred and Mollie seemed to be in a co-operative mood that summer's day.

As the buckboard made its way down Grand Avenue and towards the hotel, Jed saw ahead of him a large crowd around a big, show-style wagon, decorated with bunting and American flags. A drummer was attracting attention while another man was speaking to the crowd. "Must be one of those medicine shows," thought Jed, "when I get the milk unloaded, I'll tie the team and head over there." Medicine men were a great source of entertainment and often had wonderful things to offer the crowds. The man beating on the big bass drum announced to those within earshot that a presentation was about to be made. This practice, in the era prior to public address systems, earned salesmen the title of "drummers", and gave rise to the expression "drumming up business."

"T. W. Blumfield on the Pennington, 1895"

Suddenly the crowd, now a half block ahead of Jed, parted and a small safety bicycle appeared, traveling very quickly down Grand Avenue. The driver, his cap turned backwards, was a fit-looking man in his early twenties. Jed realized suddenly that the man wasn't pedaling, in spite of his speed, which seemed greater than Jed had ever seen a cyclist travel. He rushed past as Jed caught sight of the small fat tires and heard loud explosions coming from two tubes that jutted from behind the bicycle. Jed was impressed as he noticed dirt spurting from under the rear tire with each explosion.

Spooked by the sudden movement and loud noise from the approaching apparition, Fred and Mollie bucked and kicked, smashing the dashboard of the wagon and scattering milk cans all over the street. Jed was thrown to the ground and almost broke the other collarbone. He attempted to comfort the frightened horses to try and restrain them, but they were frantic. Two young fellows, who looked to be around fourteen, rushed to Jed's aid. One grabbed the horse's bridles, soothed them and settled them down. The other helped Jed gather up the scattered milk cans. "My pa will kill me!" sobbed Jed.

The one helping him with the cans said with a smile, "Didn't anyone ever tell you not to cry over spilt milk? I'm certain Mr. Pennington will make it right for your pa. I'm Bill Harley, and this is my pal Arthur Davidson. We live on the next block. We came to see Mr. Pennington demonstrate his *Motor Cycle*. Isn't it marvelous?" Jed had to agree, it was the most impressive thing he had ever seen. Just then, they spotted the rider of the motor cycle returning, this time pushing the machine. "Will there be another demonstration?" asked Bill. "Just as soon as I make some slight adjustments," the cyclist said behind a smile.

Jed and his new friends followed the rider back to the wagon, where a tall, distinguished looking middle-aged man was addressing the crowd with the voice of a great orator. He wore a waistcoat with a large gold watch chain across the front and a tall silk hat. "Allow me to introduce myself. I am Edward Joel Pennington, the inventor of the self-propelled vehicle. We are about to demonstrate my Pennington Motor Cycle again, once my associate, T. W. Blumfield, world champion cyclist, renews the battery on the long mingling spark ignition system. My patented *long mingling spark ignition system* broadcasts a shower of sparks throughout the combustion chambers of the twin-cylinder engine, creating the series of explosions that propels the machine at speeds in excess of a mile a minute. The Pennington motor cycle's great speed will allow it to jump across rivers and travel between cities at greater speeds than the fastest steam locomotive. Its speed knows no bounds: its only limitation being the bravery of its rider. A few short years from now, all the horses will be put out to pasture, and all travel, commercial and otherwise, will be in Pennington-designed self-propelled vehicles, powered by petroleum spirit, which comes from the ground and is limitless." Mr. Pennington stepped down from his mobile podium, while the drummer again began to beat the bass drum attracting and adding to the crowds already gathered for the show.

Mr. Pennington's associate, Blumfield, had previously removed a leather satchel from under the crossbar, replacing a telephone dry-cell battery, which he set aside. The battery was the same as the one in the phone at Jed's home. He replaced the satchel, and connected a pair of wires, which reached down the frame at the rear and somehow tied into the ends of the two tubes at the rear of the bike, which Jed now recognized as the two cylinders. The connecting rods were attached to cranks directly acting on the rear axle. After a nod from the rider, Mr. Pennington announced, "The machine will now be started and ridden at great speed! It will jump the ramp on the next block and fly like an eagle."

The cyclist began to pedal, while fiddling with a long rod, which Pennington explained, controlled the feed of the petroleum spirit. After no small effort on his behalf, the first explosion was heard, then another: the bicycle shot down the road, spraying dirt from the rear tire as before. The power was awesome. As the front wheel lifted, it appeared that the machine would flip backwards, had the long cylinders at the rear not struck the ground first. Jed's spilt milk was forgotten as he witnessed the demonstration. The little machine hit the ramp, then flew through the air and landed, rear wheel first, a measured 65 feet from the ramp, the distance having been measured personally by Pennington himself. Jed would love to have been on that machine and silently vowed to have his own motor cycle some day—and be able to travel the whole country at a mile a minute and beyond. He knew he had just witnessed history.

Once again, a now rather exhausted Blumfield pushed the machine to where Pennington stood. The demonstration concluded, Pennington got down from his perch and entered the wagon. The lettering on the sides identified it as *Thomas Kane and Company, Makers of Fine School Furniture*, which Jed recognized as being a Racine firm. Bill and Arthur suggested they had better follow Pennington and see if something could be done about the milk, and the damage to the buckboard. "Hello boys", said Pennington. When Jed explained what happened to the milk cans, Pennington said, "Nay fear, my son. By all means, bring your father with you tomorrow to our office in Racine, and I will see that your father is repaid for his trouble, with an option on Pennington stock at a reduced price, which will make him a wealthy man, and yourself a millionaire someday. This is your lucky day, Jed!"

Jed left his new friends, Bill and Arthur, who also had dreams. "Let's build a machine of our own, Art," said Bill, as they waved farewell to Jed.

Behind a rather subdued Fred and Mollie, Jed returned to the farm. All three had spent a pretty exciting day, and Jed could not wait to tell his pa about Mr. Pennington, his amazing motor cycle and the generous stock offer. While Zeke was doubtful, he reluctantly agreed to visit Pennington's office the following day.

Pennington greeted them with a flourish in his offices over Kane's factory, where there were six young ladies tapping on Underwood typewriters in the background. When Jed introduced Zeke and reminded Pennington of the milk can incident, Pennington began, "As you can see, we are writing letters to our investors all over the globe. It is a bit tedious, as there are so many different languages in use out there. Fortunately, we have a few shares of stock left." Jed was much relieved, although he wasn't sure of the meaning of stock. The only stock Jed knew of was his father's Holsteins.

"Pennington's flamboyant advertising"

Pennington went on to explain his plans to revolutionize personal transportation, and even Zeke became animated. After a half-hour, slick presentation, Pennington had a check from Zeke that would have paid for several wagonloads of milk. As the two left with dreams of great wealth, Jed noticed that one of the girls was typing gibberish, so he assumed it was one of the foreign languages Mr. Pennington was referring to. The girl next to her was typing, over and over again "The quick brown fox jumped over the lazy dog."

Both Jed and Zeke enthusiastically read of Pennington's exploits in Scientific American. Pennington exhibited the machines at the Chicago and New York cycle shows and demonstrated the bikes on the basement floor of Madison Square Gardens, as well as on the nearby streets. He, or rather his associate, took interested investors for rides on the front seat of the Pennington tandem, which supplemented the solo machine that Jed had seen. The claim was that the bikes ran on kerosene, and were good for 200 miles in an hour. The truth was that fuel was actually gasoline, and mileage was somewhat less than claimed. In addition, the design was flawed, due not as result of overheating as was postulated at the time, but because of the vagaries of the so-called, mysterious *long mingling spark ignition system* as well as the crude fuel system. No machines, other than the demo units, were produced. As the test cyclist later reported in 1931, the best trip he managed was ten miles non-stop on England's Coventry bicycle track. He always carried a pocket full of spark plugs for the long mingling spark ignition system, the obvious weak link. With a displacement of 1000cc, and a weight of less than 120 pounds, Pennington's machine performed well, but only on those rare occasions when everything was working well. Keeping the front wheel down whilst starting was another problem.

Jed had no idea that Pennington, also known as "Airbag" Pennington from a previous flying machine scam, would soon depart the USA on the quiet, after fleecing many investors. He resurfaced in England, where he repeated the whole dubious process, taking British investors for over 100,000 pounds. He built a three-wheeled automobile in England, modestly calling it the Pennington Torpedo; his detractors preferred the Pennington Raft. The Torpedo made a cameo appearance at the original London to Brighton Emancipation Run, which was held to celebrate the repeal of the Red Flag Act in England. This regulation required that a man, waving a red flag or lantern, precede all self-propelled vehicles. At the start gathering, Pennington challenged M. Leon Bollee, the young French inventor of the three-wheeler named for him, to a tug of war, and the Torpedo towed the embarrassed M. Bollee through a field in reverse. Bollee had the last laugh though, as the first three vehicles to Brighton were the dependable, little Bollee tricycles, while the Torpedo expired two miles from the start with tire trouble. None of Pennington's inventions were a commercial success, and, after returning from England and trying his scams again in the USA, he would die in obscurity in Springfield Massachusetts in 1911. Zeke's stock was worthless.

The same year, 1896, was becoming a memorable year for young Jed, as he was fortunate to witness yet another, unexpected legendary event. One June night at the dinner table, Hanna announced that she would like to visit her sister, who had recently married, in Boston. Zeke readily agreed, but, as it was not customary for ladies to travel alone on trains, he suggested Hanna take Jed to accompany her. Jed was less than keen, as he would miss some events at the bicycle club, but then a few days off school did have an appeal. Jed and Hanna boarded the train for Boston the following week.

It was the biggest place Jed had ever seen. Jed's Aunt Freda and new Uncle George were about 10 years younger than his parents. Jed quickly took to his new uncle who expressed interest in Jed's cycling and listened with interest while Jed told his story about Mr. Pennington. As it happened, Uncle George had a new safety of his own and soon had Jed riding it through the streets of Boston. On Friday of that week, George announced at the dining room table that he had borrowed a wheel from one of his friends for Jed, and that they would ride to the new Charles River bicycle track, where they would watch Mr. Sylvester Roper test a new steam-powered bicycle he had developed.

George turned out to be pretty good cyclist; he and Jed rode quickly, switching places quite a few times on the way to the track. Jed's borrowed bike was an almost new Columbia, with dropped bars and tall gearing. The ride was fun with Uncle George. George, a member of the Maryland Wheelmen, had no problem gaining entrance to the track, where he soon spotted Mr. Roper preparing for his demonstration. Naturally, Jed got as close as he could and was soon pestering Mr. Roper with questions while he made the preparations. Roper was building a fire with Franklin stove coal in the firebox of the bicycle, situated in the middle of the frame. The bicycle was a Columbia Model 36 that had been given to him by its manufacturer, Colonel A. Pope, with a commission to build a powered bicycle. The frame had been cut. As well, the pedals, cranks, and bottom bracket had been removed to accommodate a boiler, firebox, and water tank. The water tank was positioned over the boiler. Emerging from the rear was an exhaust stack, which could be rotated to a semi-vertical position when warming up and rearward when traveling. The positioning of the stack also acted as a fire-dampening device. A single cylinder double-acting engine drove the rear wheel directly. Roper explained to Jed that the engine had two pumps for water: a hand pump, and a mechanical one with a bypass valve, which fed the boiler as the bike traveled. The engine had a 2-inch bore and a 4-inch stroke. Roper, a gunsmith by trade, had used Damascus shotgun barrels as boiler tubes. Jed found this most interesting. Sylvester Roper, 76, had built several steam-powered road vehicles over his long life, including a steam-powered boneshaker in 1869—not long after the end of the Civil War. Kindly and white bearded, Sylvester Roper was the oldest man Jed had ever seen with a bicycle.

"Sylvester Roper, 1896"

Jed waited with the rest of the crowd, as Roper studied the steam gage. After about 40 minutes, Roper pulled a cord on the handlebar, and with the bike on a stand, the rear wheel began to spin. He explained he was clearing the steam cylinder of condensed water, while warming up the engine. He pushed the bicycle off the stand, mounted it and began to circulate the half-mile track in eerie silence. George got out his pocket watch and timed the laps as Roper gathered speed. Jed could see the glow on the track surface from the coals in the grate below the firebox, and, as the bike gathered speed, red-hot cinders blew out the stack. An almost inaudible *chuff-chuff* sound of a steam locomotive could be heard from the forced draft smokestack. Two very fit cyclists were following Roper as he made the first lap of the track, but before that lap was finished and Roper built up speed, they had dropped well behind.

"Forty-six seconds," said an exited George after the first lap. "And look how he's pulled away from the cyclists. John and Harold, two of our fastest boys, are pedaling like the very devil" As the second lap finished, George jumped up and hollered, "Thirty-three seconds! He'll hit a mile-a-minute or more if he keeps up the pace!"

About a third of the way into the next lap, and traveling even faster, Roper suddenly slumped forward over the water tank; a deadly pallor covering his elderly features. The front wheel began to wobble; suddenly, the machine crashed, leaving Roper tumbling along the track alongside his bicycle. Jed and George rushed forward with others to offer help, while Roper and his cycle remained motionless. After examining Roper, a doctor in the crowd announced to the hushed assembly that Sylvester Roper was dead.

George and Jed pushed the cycle to the side of the track and leaned it against the fence. Jed noticed the steam gage was still showing 120 pounds, so he opened the blow-down valve to release the pressure. This maneuver came naturally, after the time spent around the threshing engine at the farm. One disaster was enough for the day, without an explosion.

On the way home from Boston, Jed was dull company for his mother. He was thinking about the kindly old Mr. Roper and his marvelous machine and mourning his passing. Sylvester Roper had suffered a heart attack while riding the bike; he was the first motorcycle fatality in history.

Chapter Three

Wisconsin and Boston
1899-1904

Jed's trips to Boston with Hanna became annual affairs. Jed had become very fond of his Uncle George. A wealthy man with a successful shipping business, George doted on his young nephew. Aunt Freda proved to be a good cook and made sure that Jed was well satisfied, especially upon returning from long rides with Uncle George. As he had just bought a new Orient, George gave Jed his old Columbia safety, making Jed pretty much up to date in terms of bicycle needs. The Columbia safety followed Jed and his mother, back and forth, on the Boston trips in the freight car.

During the July of 1899 Boston trip, George and Jed cycled to the Charles River bicycle track again—the site of Sylvester Roper's final ride. George had another surprise in store for Jed. "There is a new type of bicycle racing taking place. We have two visiting teams coming with motor pacers. The motorized pacing tandem leads the racers, so the bicycles following in the draft of the machine can get up to higher speeds. I know you will be interested in those contraptions!" said Uncle George with a wink.

They found the tandem pacers at the track surrounded by a large crowd gathered around them. Jed was surprised to see one that was built by the same manufacturer as George's bicycle, the Waltham Manufacturing Company of Waltham Massachusetts—the name, *Orient*, prominent on its headstock badge. The Waltham name was familiar to Jed; it was the same as that on the mantle clock at home. George and Jed wasted no time in introducing themselves to the two operators of the tandem. The rider, who sat in front, was a well-known bicycle racer named Charles Henshaw, while the engineer sitting in the rear to operate the engine was another well-known cyclist. His name would become more famous in time. "Hello, Jed," he said with a smile, "My name is Oscar Hedstrom." Jed recognized the accent spoken by this lean gentleman as Swedish.

"Henshaw and Hedstrom Tandem, 1899"

Hedstrom explained the workings of the tandem. "The engine is a French DeDion Bouton. Count DeDion has developed the first practical air-cooled engine, small enough to be attached to bicycle frames. The petroleum spirit is held in this triangular tank. As the descending piston opens the intake valve, fumes are drawn off the surface of the fuel and piped with air to the combustion chamber. We call the device a surface carburetor. Carburetor is a French word coined by Count DeDion to describe a device for mixing air with fuel. The fuel is fired by a spark plug, which is controlled from this timer here. The spark is made with a telephone battery and a high-tension coil. As the engineer, it's my job to control the mixture of the fuel and air by operating these two air valves and also to inject oil into the engine for lubrication, as required. I also have to watch the bicycles behind us to make sure we keep ahead of them, but stay close enough that they can take advantage of the draft we generate. Mr. Henshaw here, steers the machine, and makes sure we stay on track."

"Stanley Lococycle, 1899"

The second pacer, the "Lococycle," was built by identical black-bearded twins from the Locomobile Company, FE and FO Stanley. Their machine was an awe-inspiring device with a 14" boiler, a huge water tank above and two large vertical tanks at the rear for compressed air and fuel. On the side of this 800 pound cycle were the words "On, Stanley, On!" Eddie McDuffy, who hoped, this very day, to establish a new world speed record following in its wake, had commissioned the steamer. Remembering the performance of Sylvester Roper's little 120-pound steam cycle in 1896, Jed and George had great expectations for this one.

The Lococycle gurgled and boiled and, with much fanfare, steamed away, with McDuffy hot on its tail. It wasn't long before the machine slowed, and McDuffy, showing disgust, passsed the pacer. The problem was apparently with the burner, as both Stanleys could be seen fiddling with it, and both had soot covered faces from backfires from the firebox. McDuffy was unable to achieve the record he wanted; the Stanley's were left with the problem. Jed and George reflected that Sylvester Roper's coal-fire system had been simpler and trouble free.

Henshaw and Hedstrom began to pedal their pacer. It soon started with a chuff-chuff sound, much noisier than the Lococycle, or Roper's steam cycle had been, but smoother and with less mechanical violence than Jed remembered from Pennington's motor cycle demonstration. Quite a bit of blue smoke came from the exhaust: Jed wasn't sure he would like to be the cyclists following in that acrid smoke. The lap times were faster than Jed had ever seen from cyclists, proving that the pacer certainly increased their speeds.

There were a total of six races that day. Three had to be restarted because of breakdowns with the pacers: one flat tire and two engine failures, the second of which was terminal, so that the last race was held without the pacer. According to Jed's new friend, Mr. Hedstrom, the engine had broken an exhaust valve, and he'd used his last spare the day before. "We learn from our breakdowns, Jed. The more we work on them, the better these machines will be in the future." Deep in thought, he was examining the broken parts and the cylinder head, when Jed and George made their departure.

Uncle George commented that the pacers might be more hindrance than help, due to their frequent breakdowns. For an answer, Jed thought back to the charismatic Pennington, who claimed travel between cities would be done on motor cycles faster than the speediest locomotives. "With clever fellows like Mr. Hedstrom working on them, they will get better," Jed ventured.

As they raced back to George and Freda's home, Jed was wishing his Columbia had some sort of engine, allowing him to double his speed or better than that. Wouldn't it be terrific, he thought, if he could return on roads to Racine, traveling at a mile a minute on two wheels, instead of riding on the train? Jed was unaware as to just how rough those roads would be compared to the rail line. Even if such a futuristic machine existed, there would be very few places to ride that fast.

Feb 29ᵗʰ 1900 was another birthday for Jed, his fourth. "We've gotten you a major gift this year and your uncle George and I have chipped in together. It's out in the driving shed. Happy Birthday, son." said Zeke.

Jed rushed out to the shed. He couldn't believe his eyes: it was a motor cycle! And, on its rear-mounted fuel tank in gold leaf lettering on shiny dark green paint, was the name, *Orient*. The whole machine was decorated in gold pin striping. In the envelope attached to the handlebars, Jed found a letter from Uncle George.

> "Dear Jed," it read. "Your father and I have been discussing this for some time via mail. Oscar Hedstrom who you have met, has done some work with Charles Metz of Orient, and has helped in the development of this new single seat two-wheeled machine. This is one of the very first produced. Your pa and I decided that there is a new century starting, and a young man such as yourself will see many new things, particularly in the area of two-wheeled transportation, which seems to fascinate you so much. This Orient is the first commercially produced machine of its type in the USA, and hopefully it will teach you new things, take you to new places, and perhaps lead you to a new career. We know you are not big on 'book learning' but neither were your pa or I, but we've both done OK. Happy fourth birthday, sixteen year old! Uncle George"

The envelope also included an instruction book detailing the operation of the bike. Zeke had thoughtfully picked up a gallon can of petroleum spirit at the drug store along with a new telephone battery for the ignition. Both items sat beside the machine. His father interrupted the boy's thoughts, "As you can see, Jed, there is a stand under the rear wheel. George suggested that you might want to start the engine, get used to the controls and so forth. There is some oil here on the shelf." Riding the bike right now was hardly an option in February with the roads chocked with snow.

The Orient was a very tall machine. Fortunately, Jed was already a tall boy at six-foot—two. Even at this, it was obvious that he would be unable to reach the ground while sitting on the seat, which was over 40 inches above the floor. He would have to push off and hop aboard, much as with his old Star bicycle. There were extended axle nuts at the rear to help with stepping up.

The engine was a DeDion Bouton, much like the one he had seen in the pacing tandem, but the manual made reference to "improved valves." Could this be one of Mr. Hedstrom's contributions? The triangular surface carburetor was replaced with an instrument identified as a "Longuemare Carburetor." It had a float bowl on the side along with two levers controlled from rods to the crossbar. Marked "air" and "gaz," this was understandable French.

After attaching the battery and after putting the various fluids in place, Jed soon had the engine running smoothly. He spent hours over the next few days becoming familiar with the procedures of starting, running and oiling the new machine. After a few days of this, and with the aid of Zeke's tools, Jed dismantled, and then reassembled the engine, not just once but three times. He soon had a complete understanding of the various parts, their functions and how they operated. The snows were deep that year; for Jed, it would be a long wait for spring and clear roads.

When the snows finally receded, Jed pushed the Orient out onto the road one day in late March. He had run the engine outside the driving shed with the bike still on the stand to get things warmed up, as recommended in the little instruction book. Leaving the stand, behind, Jed wheeled the machine out. (Stands that folded and stayed with motorcycles were yet to be invented, as were fenders.) Jake ran with the bike, mounted it by stepping on the little extensions on the rear axle nuts, and began pedaling furiously. The engine started, and Jed was propelled down the road with the power pulses of the 2¼ HP engine. All in a matter of seconds, his excitement turned to concern, then dread, as mud from the front wheel soon splattered in his eyes. The road was very muddy from the recent spring run off. Jed went into a long reverse-lock slide with the engine still racing. In all the excitement, procedures were forgotten. Jed slid on his face through the mud, while the Orient slid off in another direction. Within seconds, Jed had experienced both his first ride, and his first accident.

"Glory be to Peter!" exclaimed Hanna as Jed returned, pushing the bike past the house to the driving shed. "Don't you dare come in this house looking like that! Take those clothes off and wash yourself in the horse trough!" Jed did just that, but not before setting the Orient back on its stand, and thoroughly cleaning the mud from it. Fortunately, the mud was soft and gooey enough, that the shiny green paint and gold trim were as good as new.

Once the roads dried, Jed was back out with the bike and soon mastered the machine. Each time he rode it, he traveled farther, then farther still. On a regular basis, Jed was soon riding to Milwaukee, a big city 40 miles from the farm. In Milwaukee, Jed visited many places of interest, not the least of which was the hardware store that sold Orient motorcycles. Jed soon made friends with the proprietor, Arthur Kane. As it turned out, Kane was cousin of the Thomas Kane, who owned the school furniture business in Racine, and had helped bankroll Pennington. Arthur was looking for someone to help him with the motorcycle sales, and Jed found himself with a job offer.

Jed's job was not all motorcycles; he was required to help in the hardware store as well, sweeping the floor and doing other menial tasks. Jed loved it though, as he could talk motorcycles all he wished. The crafty Mr. Kane had "Arthur Kane & Company" gold leafed on the battery box of Jed's Orient, even though it had come from an agent in Boston, a friend of his Uncle George. Jed could care less, as he was now an employed adult. This was fine with Zeke and Hanna; recognizing that he was not a farmer at heart, they wished their son well in his new endeavors. Zeke had two hired men now, so all was well at the farm. Was Jed a spoiled boy? Surprisingly, he was not, in spite of being the only child of a modestly wealthy family and having a childless aunt and uncle who also doted on him. Life was good for Jed. He soon found a rooming house in Milwaukee and was living on his own.

While motor vehicles appeared on the streets of the city in 1900, they were infrequently seen. Horseless carriages, such as the curved dash Olds, and occasionally the odd big French Panhard, or German Mercedes would appear. These were cars famous for racing exploits in the USA and abroad, particularly the Vanderbilt Cup series. Horses still provided most of the transportation motive power, gradually becoming accustomed to the clattering, smoking, noisy, contraptions in the city. Outside town, and when riding out to see his parents, Jed had to be constantly alert. With few powered vehicles in use, he often spooked horses, causing a great deal of distain from other users of the road. What didn't help, was his fitment of an exhaust cut-out on his aging Orient, to make it as fast as the newer models. Shortly after Jed's bike was built, Orient abandoned the DeDion Bouton engine in favor of the French Aster engines, some of which had almost twice the displacements of Jed's 2¼ HP model. As he was unable to afford a new machine each year, Jed was becoming a "tuner," a term that would not be used for a few years hence. He was confounded by the speed in which the early motorcycles became obsolete through rapid developments.

In 1902, Jed convinced Art Kane to help him financially for an endurance run to be held between Boston and New York City, the first event of its type to be held on the continent. He was able to convince Kane that he had a good chance of doing well, which would help sales. Expenses would be minimal, as he would stay with his aunt and uncle in Boston while preparing for the event. Jed planned to return by train from the finish in New York, after receiving the trophies, fame and money he was hoping for. Kane telegraphed Waltham Manufacturing, and was assured of limited factory support for Jed. This was unusual for a relatively unknown such as Jed. However, as one of the largest sellers of Waltham Clocks in the eastern United States, Kane Hardware had the motorcycle dealership as well. Neither a cyclist nor motorcyclist, Arthur Kane had come to depend on Jed.

Jed arrived in Boston on July 1ˢᵗ 1902, unloaded the big Orient from the freight car and headed to George and Freda's luxurious home on Atlantic Avenue. He carried a satchel containing spark plugs, a couple of valves, two inner tubes, a patching kit, some PDQ tire casing plugs, a small roll of fence wire, an extra drive belt, and a few basic tools—in addition to his clothes. He felt well prepared for the adventure ahead.

Aunt Freda had her cook prepare a big meal for her favorite, and only, nephew. When Uncle George offered him a cigar afterwards, Jed declined, as he'd tried that before, becoming as sick as a dog. George took Jed out to the carriage house to show Jed his two latest toys. The first was an automobile, a 1902 Locomobile. George admired the silence of steam power, claiming that it was a less fearful apparition to horses than an internal combustion car, but the clouds of condensing steam exhaust was really about as bad. The best part of Locomobile ownership according to George was starting. "There is no twirling required," said George. "All you need to do is light the thing. My New York office manager had a heart attack last month twirling the engine of his Oldsmobile."

Of far more interest to Jed, was George's brand new Indian. Oscar Hedstrom, and another cyclist, George Hendee, had launched the Hendee Manufacturing Company the year prior in Springfield Massachusetts. Their little Indians were selling like hotcakes. Cast into the crankcase of the single-cylinder engine were the words "The Hedstrom Motor." An unusual feature, was the all chain drive, as most other machines at the time featured belt drive. The bike appeared tiny in comparison to the Orient, and Jed wasn't overly impressed until George fired it up and let Jed have a go the following day. To his dismay, Jed discovered that the little Indian was as fast as the Orient, and due to its size, quite a bit easier to ride. He began to wonder how many riders would be riding Indians in the endurance run. He would find out on the fourth of July.

"Orient on Boston-NY endurance run 1902"

On the morning of the fourth, Jed rode his Orient to City Hall, which was close by, while George and Freda followed in the Locomobile. George had left his Indian sitting in the carriage house, having concluded that he was getting a bit too old for this kind of foolishness. He and Freda decided they would take the train to New York to see the finish the following day, when the three of them would top the day off with a nice dinner, and a stay at the Plaza Hotel.

"Ocsar Hedstrom with his Indian 1902"

By start time, thirty-one motorcyclists had assembled at City Hall. There were several Orients like Jed's, but all had Aster engines. There were several Indians, two of which were being ridden by Oscar Hedstrom and George Hendee. Mr. E. R. Thomas of Buffalo, New York, was present, providing encouragement for the three gentlemen riding his "Thomas Auto Bi's." One of the riders was Charles Henshaw, who had been Oscar Hedstrom's cycling partner on the Orient tandem pacer that Jed had seen back in 1899. Among other first-hand sponsors was George Holley, riding one of his Holley motorcycles. The Holley, like the Indian, featured a chain drive, but was direct, unlike the Indian, which had a countershaft. The crankcase formed the bottom of its diamond frame in place of the bottom bracket of a bicycle. The bottom bracket and pedal cranks were attached forward of the engine, while the cylinder occupied the normal location of the seat tube. All the machines entered had pedal start, and all were direct drive with no clutch. Jed recognized most of the riders as well-known pedal cyclists.

The Metropole Cycling Club which organized the event, wisely called it an "Endurance Run," as they had no wish to curry any bad press such as surrounded events like the Vanderbilt Cup Series, held on public roads in Europe, where accidents and carnage involving spectators were well publicized. As the riders were flagged off though, it became evident that this was indeed going to be a race. Such is the way with young men.

The distance to New York was 254 miles, to be done in two sections. The rules called for a maintained minimum speed of 8 mph, but 15 mph was the maximum allowable. The first day's ride ended at Hartford Connecticut, a distance of 125 miles. Anyone not getting that far in 15.6 hours would be disqualified after the first day. A rider arriving in Hartford in under 8-1/3 hours, would be disqualified for traveling too fast. There was very little risk of that.

Except for one stubborn Thomas, all the riders got a good start and motored quickly down State Street, towards the outskirts of town, to head south. Jed's uncle, after seeing Jed safely away, assisted Mr. E.R. Thomas push George Henshaw's stubborn machine. It turned out that a battery wire had come loose, and poor Henshaw was pretty exhausted from pedaling before the problem was solved. His flooded engine finally started, he took off after the others, all of whom had disappeared in clouds of dust.

Jed found himself in the middle of the pack, just behind George Hendee. The dust became worse as the city houses gave way to bush and farm fields. It was very difficult to keep the machines upright, as the clay surface road, as hard as concrete, had large ruts from the horse drawn vehicles, the norm for this time. About three miles into the race, George Hendee caught a rut on his Indian and fell, sliding the bike sideways. Jed cut his ignition and stopped by the prone Mr. Hendee. "Are you OK sir?" asked Jed. "Don't worry about me, son. I'll be soon passing you on my much superior Indian," said Hendee with a grin. Jed pedaled off, and by now found himself to be at the tail end of the group. Sure enough, in another mile, as Jed was struggling through a badly rutted section, Hendee passed him on the Indian, giving a little wave as he did so. Jed worked on adjustments to his timing and carburetion: he felt the Orient surge ahead and overtake two of the slower machines, a Thomas, and an obsolete, just two-year-old, Marsh, which had an engine smaller than Jed's Orient.

The Orient was making pretty good time down the straight road, soon passing an Indian that was misfiring, when he saw Hendee ahead of him by 200 yards. Jed had experimented considerably with the Orient, based upon his experience with the earlier model. Nearly all the engines of the period were four stroke singles, with automatic intake valves. Most had an intake-over-exhaust configuration. The two-stroke engine, although in production, was not popular; there were none on the reliability trial. The automatic intake valves that were used in these four stroke singles had weak springs and no cam operating them. They were depended upon the suction caused by the descending piston during the intake stroke to open them. If the springs were too weak, the engines would not run quickly; conversely, if the springs were too strong, the engines would only run well at high speeds, and sometimes would not start at all until spun over very quickly. Jed had his tuned for speed.

This proved to be a disadvantage, as they came to the first long hill. As the engine slowed, some "LPA" (light pedal assistance) was often required—earlier in Jed's case than with some others. Because the pedaling gear was low to provide power for starting the engines, as well moving the bike forward, this pedal assistance was, essentially, a lot of work. Jed had youth on his side, but by the time he'd crested the hill, Hendee was well out of site, and the Indian he'd passed earlier had overtaken him as well. On the way down the hill he made better time, Jed realized that the large diameter 28 inch wheels on the Orient gave him a slight advantage on the rough surface, through which rocks poked up here and there. Near the bottom, he passed the second Indian again; the rider had come to grief upon hitting one of those rocks. The cane (hickory) rim on the front of the Indian had split, resulting in tire rolling off and becoming entangled in the front forks, throwing the rider over the handlebars. Fortunately, he got to his feet quickly, apparently unhurt, and gave Jed the thumbs-up sign as he charged past. That Indian was likely out of the event. Jed was pleased to have steel rims on the Orient.

At this stage, Jed was on his own for about a half mile and wasn't sure where he was in the lineup, but suspected correctly that he was near the rear. Rounding a corner, Jed came close to colliding with Hendee and a Metz rider, who were picking up their bikes and yelling profanities at one another. The Metz appeared to have a smashed front wheel, and bent forks. Half a mile later, Jed was overtaken by Hendee once more. This time there was no friendly wave from the determined Indian rider, whose shiny new steed already was looking somewhat the worse for wear.

Jed motored on again for a while without seeing anyone else, apart from a horse and buggy with a team of very skittish horses and a driver shaking his fist at Jed. Obviously the damage had been done, so Jed simply waved as he blasted by at over 20 mph. "She's really on the boil now," Jed thought to himself as he bounced along the rough road, fighting to hang onto the bucking machine. Already he could feel his aching back and his kidneys, which were taking a terrible pounding. Suddenly he hit a rock; his front tire went flat, rolling off the rim right away. As he slowed down, he watched the tire roll along with the wheel, flipping from one side of the wheel to the other until he stopped. He considered himself very lucky that the tire had not tangled in the front forks, as had happened with the Indian a few miles back.

The canvas tire had a hole in the casing; Jed had casing plugs, which now came in handy. He pushed the red rubber plug through the white tire from the inside and replaced the tube with a spare he was carrying. During this, he removed the intake valve pod from the engine and removed the shim he had fashioned to strengthen the spring. He decided it would be better to sacrifice a little speed in exchange for enhanced hill climbing ability. Jed was soon on the road once more. He noticed a bit of a thump from the casing plug, a minor inconvenience in comparison to the roughness of the hard clay.

As another large hill came into view, Jed could see eight or nine riders struggling up the slope. It was the steepest he had experienced so far; Jed noticed that five of the cyclists had dismounted their machines and were pushing them. The approach was rough and Jed had his machine going as fast as he dared. As the engine slowed, Jed began to pedal as fast as he could, before the engine lost power. Pedaling furiously, he listened to the engine slow down as it labored up the hill. Jed had also pulled back a notch on the belt tightener for greater purchase. With a final exhausted effort, Jed reached the crest of the hill. Not noticing Hendee on the hill, Jed concluded he was still ahead. He now knew he wasn't last though, as he had passed five machines on the hill, by standing up and pedaling with all his might.

Jed took off down the far side of the hill at breakneck speed and was soon bouncing from side to side, nearly losing control of the bike again in the hard, dry and rutted clay. The Orient, like all the other motorcycles in this event, had no suspension of any kind, front or rear—just very limited springs in the hard bicycle saddles. At the bottom, the roadway smoothed out for a while, allowing Jed to enjoy the scenery of Massachusetts. Things were slightly easier now; he hadn't passed any machines since that particularly tough hill. He was soon upon the village of Southbridge, where locals were cheering along the streets, and followed the signs posted by the Metropole Cycling Club to the first fuel stop, the drug store. A dozen machines were lined up, and Jed noticed Hedstrom's Indian being replenished at the head of the queue. It was a slow process, as the lone apothecary slowly filtered petroleum spirit, or naphtha, through cloth, measuring the liquid with a glass graduate. No one seemed to mind though: they were tired and welcomed the rest, sandwiches and Moxie soft drinks supplied by the club. Hendee was three machines ahead of Jed in the lineup. By the time Jed's Orient was being filled, he had two riders behind him. He wondered about the other three or four he'd passed on that hill.

The afternoon went much the same as the morning. The roads were dry and rutted, but the scenery was marvelous and the weather was perfect for this adventure. He traded places with a couple of other bikes, a Thomas and an Indian, but otherwise gained nothing on other riders, other than another Orient where the engine appeared to be coming apart. That rider was out of the race. This prompted Jed to see to the oiling of his engine.

The fuel stop at Southbridge had been the only one of the day, as those early machines were easy on naphtha. Most averaged 60 to 80 miles per gallon, due to their light weight and low power. Most machines, including Jed's, were fitted with fuel tanks slightly larger than standard. Some riders carried pocket hip flasks with a little extra, just in case, although this was frowned upon. The event was run as a reliability trial, providing a showcase for the practicability of the motorcycle, with full factory support from several manufacturers. More than one rider carried a hip flask of corn, rather than petroleum spirit, to ease the pain of the ride.

On the trip from Southbridge, he did not pass any riders, but did see several that had broken down or fallen on the rough roads, including Hendee once more. Finally arriving in Hartford, to the cheers of locals lining the streets, the riders checked into a comfortable hotel after reaching the day's finish on the street out front. Jed discovered that he was 15th of a total of 18 still remaining. It had taken him 12½ hours to cover the 125 miles, thereby averaging an even 10 mph. Thirteen other riders had broken down, or had accidents, and were out of the race. One unfortunate had been bucked off his Thomas and had landed on his head, knocking himself out cold. After a steak dinner, Jed fell into bed exhausted. The motorcycles were locked in the compound behind the hotel, and riders were denied access to them. One of the rules of the event was that all maintenance must be done during the timed event. The night's rest was a time out for all.

The following morning at the pre-sun-up breakfast of eggs and sausages, George Hendee, who'd finished behind Jed, told the group that he had suffered a total of 8 spills that day. Looking around the table, Jed realized that he was amongst a group of very famous cyclists and that he was lucky to have got as far as he had. Hendee was about the same age as his uncle George, and like George, was a bit heavy set, probably having gained a bit of weight due to the good life. Oscar Hedstrom, also one of the older riders, was lean and fit; he had come in a creditable fourth at the end of the first day.

As the group went out to the compound to retrieve their steeds, they faced a new problem—rain. The starters waved the machines off in the same order they had arrived the previous day, and at the same time intervals. Jed had a long wait. The leather belts on the belt drive bikes were wet, and slippage was a big problem in starting, so fellow riders helped push the machines. It was tough work, and by the time Jed was waved away, he felt he had done the work of another day's ride. Fortunately, as the number of riders diminished, local cycling enthusiasts filled in for them, and two strong boys helped push Jake's Orient. Every time he dropped the valve lifter, the engine quit turning, and the belt slipped hopelessly. He pulled the lever back as far as he dared; finally the tightened belt took hold, and the engine started. It slipped while power was put on, but slowly improved as the friction dried the leather. Jake had noticed that this was no problem with the chain drive machines such as the Indians.

With the rain just beginning, the clay surfaces of the roads were still fairly hard. Jed was going well, but was again soon overtaken by Hendee. This time there was a wave from the older rider, who had a renewed respect for the young cyclist. A few miles outside of town, the skies opened up, and the road was soon a mass of sticky mud, some of the worst Jed had experienced. The bike slithered around, splattering Jed with mud, but he was lucky to have the new-fangled motoring goggles his Uncle George had bought for him. It was only a matter of time though, before he slid, splattering down the road on his face. The bike had fallen on the left side and, as it slid along, the belt and its pulleys became well fouled with the sticky gumbo. Yesterday, they were plagued with that other sticky material that was a hazard to pioneer motorcyclists, horse manure, but mud was far more plentiful today. Jed picked up a stick, and began to clear his wheels and belt drive system. After righting the bike, Jed tried pedaling and starting; again he was plagued by a wet slipping belt. Finally, the engine fired, and once again Jed slithered down the road ahead.

Another hill loomed ahead, but this time, because of the muddy conditions and the wet, slipping belt, Jed was forced to throw in the towel half way up. Jed pushed, and along with four other riders, struggled up the hill, slipping in the mud and dropping the bike several times before he reached the crest. Exhausted, he looked to the southwest, and saw sunshine. Things were definitely looking up.

Coasting down the hill made for an easy start; the engine soon started with minimum effort on Jed's part, as he headed towards the fuel stop at Danbury. With fewer riders, the fuel up was less crowded than the last one; he took advantage of the extra vittles and Moxie drinks and, with a full belly, fired up and headed southwest towards New York. The roads were much better on this last stretch, and at one point, he even passed a horse-drawn grader improving the surface. Approaching the big city, Jed saw no other bikes. He noticed that the urban area began even before he got to the East River; Jed was to cross at the Williamsburg Bridge.

Jed couldn't believe its size as he began to cross the Williamsburg Bridge; he gazed in wonderment as a huge four-funneled ocean liner steamed underneath him. Ahead were the wonders of the big city. Suddenly, Jed heard a large bang and clatter, and as he coasted to the rail of the bridge. He then realized that in his excitement of nearing the finish, and gawking at the sites, he had forgotten to oil the engine. Stopping, he realized that for him, the run was over: the crankcase had split, and a broken connecting rod poked through the front. Jed had made it to New York, but was out of the race nevertheless. He was unable to ride to the finish. Dejected, he pushed his machine the rest of the way across the bridge, wandering aimlessly with it into the streets of Manhattan.

Pushing the bike through the streets, Jed saw sights and heard sounds he had never before experienced. He heard unfamiliar languages and strange, broken English. He suddenly realized he was lost and needed help. Just then, he had to step aside to allow the passage of a large wagon, driven by a strange-looking man with a wide black hat, long hair and a beard with ringlets down the side of his face, not unlike those of his aunt Freda, except his were certainly not blonde like hers. "Rags, Bones and Bottles!" shouted the man, with a strange accent. "Sir, I need some help!" hollered Jed. "So, what's your problem, already? You have that new fangled machine, and all I have is this broken down old horse and wagon," said the man.

Jed spilled out the story of the reliability run, the fact that his new fangled machine was broken, and said he was lost. "Do you know the way to the Plaza Hotel?" asked Jed. "I'd be glad to pay you to take me and my bike there." The little, middle-aged man looked at Jed with a smile and replied, "While the Plaza Hotel is not on my normal route, I would like to hear more of your adventures, young fellow. You can tell me on the way to the Plaza. There will be no charge."

Jed and his new companion, who introduced himself as Remus Bernbaum, loaded the Orient into the wagon, and headed down Broadway, with Jed relating his adventures along the way. Jed invited Remus to join him, and to meet the other cyclists. Bernbaum declined with a smile, as they unloaded the Orient, saying, "I don't think I would be welcome at the Plaza, Jed. Anyway, I must take care of my business. Shalom!" As Jed waved to the retreating wagon, Jed realized he'd been talking so much he'd forgotten to get Bernbaum's story. It was probably far more interesting than his own. He was unaware he'd met an Orthodox Jew who'd come through Ellis Island ten years prior, escaping a pogrom in Russia. It was Remus Bernbaum, and other immigrants like him, that gave New York the cosmopolitan flavor, making it one of the world's most interesting cities.

As Jed turned towards the Plaza, he noticed a gathering of his fellow competitors, laughing uproariously at his arrival. "You are the only one who's finished the run in a *sheeny* wagon," said one. Jed, unaware of the slight towards Remus, went inside to join the others. They were in the Plaza's very elegant bar, and some were already well into their cups. Uncle George was there, paying for the drinks and enjoying the camaraderie. Aunt Freda had retired to their room to rest from the train ride. "Here's your room key, Jed. You've got a room all to yourself."

"Finish at the Plaza Hotel, 1902"

Jed discovered that thirteen riders had finished in New York. Jed had technically arrived there, but was not one of the fortunate thirteen. Seven of the fourteen riders had perfect scores of 1000 points and received awards. The first four machines reaching New York were George Holley's Holley, O. L. Pickard's Indian, L. H. Roberts Orient, and N. P. Bernard's Crescent. George Hendee had fallen off fourteen times in total. Hedstrom had faired much better as one of the seven with perfect scores.

As they sat with their drinks, Jed with his third beer, Oscar Hedstrom said, "You look a bit dejected, young Jed. You shouldn't, you know. You came close to finishing with an excellent score, and you are the youngest of riders. Eighteen years of age, isn't it?" asked Hedstrom.

"I've had only four birthdays, sir, as I was born on the 29th of February, but I've wrecked my engine," said Jed. "The bike was a present from my father and Uncle George here, and I can't afford to fix it.

"Write down your address, Jed. I don't usually help the competition," Hedstrom said with a smile, "but I happen to have a DeDion engine at the factory that I did some experimenting with while developing the Hedstrom motor. I will send it to you as a present. Don't you dare tell anyone where you got it! All I ask is that when you can afford a new bike you consider the best of the lot, an Indian." This comment caused groans from the riders of the other makes.

Jed felt much better after that kindness from Hedstrom and accepted another beer. He had no recollection the following morning of how he got to bed, but he got there somehow. His head was pounding in the morning. Motorcycling was a tough business.

After saying goodbye to his fellow competitors and relatives Jed returned home the following day by train with the damaged Orient in the baggage car. On arriving in Milwaukee, he had to push the bike back to his rooming house. If Oscar Hedstrom kept his promise of that other engine, the effort of the reliability trial was well worthwhile. He'd seen some wonderful countryside, and developed a wanderlust that he realized was within his reach aboard his motorcycle.

Kane was pleased that Jed had made it to New York, but shared the disappointment over the unsuccessful finish. Jed was quickly back to work, helping in the hardware store, while selling and servicing the Orients that were sold from there.

In two weeks time, a small crate arrived for Jed at the railroad station. In it was the promised DeDion motor from Oscar Hedstrom of the Hendee Manufacturing Company. Jed opened the crate at Kane's, where he kept his Orient, and soon had the new engine installed in the frame. Before he did so, though, he compared the two engines. With the cylinders removed, Jed discovered that Hedstrom had filled in some areas in the head to raise the compression ratio higher than the original and had fitted it with slightly larger valves. More importantly even than that, was the discovery that both the bore and the stroke were increased as well. The DeDion was now a 3½ HP engine. Jed could hardly wait to see how it went. He was pleased to discover that it was more than a match for the new Orients he was selling, which were now fitted with Aster engines from France, and equal as well to those fitted to the new Orient built engines that appeared in the fall of that year.

CHAPTER FOUR

CHANGES AT HOME

Jed took many rides on the Orient around the area that summer, traveling as far as he could on his days off. He soon had more days off than on, as sales and service slowed down in the fall; he moved back home to help on the farm that winter with the promise of his job back in the spring.

One December morning, while helping Zeke and the two hired men milk the Holsteins, Jed heard a crash and the clang of a milk pail being overturned a couple of cows away. He rushed over to find his father lying on the floor. "I have a very bad pain in my chest, Jed. You'd better help me to the house and let the boys finish with the milking." Jed helped his father to the house and onto the couch in the parlor. Jed saw the same deadly pallor on his father's face as he'd seen on Sylvester Roper's when he fell off his steam bicycle. By the time Doc Hanson arrived, all he could do was pronounce Zeke dead of an apparent heart attack.

The Flemings were devastated by Zeke's sudden demise. He had not been sick a day in his life, then suddenly, he had been taken from them. He was only 55 years of age.

At the very large funeral, the owner of the farm next door approached Hanna and told her he would be glad to purchase the farm should she find it too difficult to handle on her own. The neighbor was well aware that the son was not all that interested in taking over; in this he was correct. George and Freda also spoke to her, putting some gentle pressure on her to move to Boston to live with them. Their house was huge, and as Freda said, "You'd love Boston, Hanna." George and Freda also knew that Jed wouldn't make much of a farmer. No decisions were made at that time. Jed willingly took over the operation, but by the spring he was hankering for two-wheeled adventure again. He got out on the bike when he could, but there was very little time for extended trips.

The owner of the neighboring farm, a widower, became a frequent visitor at the Fleming farm. He was very helpful with advice, which Jed appreciated, because he lacked the expertise of his father, and Hanna had had little to do with the daily running of the place. It came as a bit of a surprise, however, when

Harold and Hanna announced their betrothal in the spring of 1903. They were to be married in the fall.

Meanwhile, this left Arthur Kane on his own selling Orients that year, although Jed made himself available when he had spare time, but it was not often. In late summer, when Jed went by the hardware store on his machine, Kane showed him a letter from Waltham Manufacturing. It stated that the company had decided to suspend the production of motorcycles. It was also announced that Charles H. Metz, the designer responsible for the motorcycle, had resigned. Arthur also had a letter from the same Charles Metz announcing the creation of the Charles H. Metz Co., and the plans to produce a new ma chine. "Are you going to take on the new motorcycle of Mr. Metz?" asked Jed hopefully. "If not, maybe we could get an Indian agency! I know Mr. Hedstrom there."

"Forget it, Jed. I never really had much interest in this motorcycle business. I'd rather just be back selling Waltham's time pieces. It's a relief, actually, particularly as you are not around much to help me, now that you have taken up farming," smiled Kane. "You did a great job for me though. I'm stuck with a bunch of parts for that old Orient of yours, so consider them yours. It should keep that contraption going for a while. You can keep the stuff in the basement here, until you need it."

Jed didn't have a lot of time for his motorcycle in 1903, but took it out whenever he could. Now that his mother was engaged, he saw more of his future father-in-law than ever, as well as his two sons, one of whom was married with two children of his own. The second son was "born simple," as the saying went at the time. Although he could do simple tasks, he would never be up to the job of running the operation. Both Wilson families and the unmarried son lived in Harold's home, which was larger than the Fleming's. Jed's future father-in-law, Harold, gradually took control of the running of the Fleming farm; Jed's status was reduced to that of another hired hand. The two farms together became a major operation.

Jed accepted this eventuality: his mother seemed to be happy, and Harold Wilson was a fair taskmaster, although he obviously favored his own two boys. Jed decided that, as soon as he could afford it, he would get out on his own and "seek his fortune."

A trans-continental motorcycle attempt had begun by On May 16th of 1903. Jed followed its progress with great interest in the pages of *The Motorcycle Magazine,* something he eagerly awaited when it was published on the 15th of each month. George Wyman of California, a 26-year-old cyclist, had set out on motorcycle to travel from San Francisco to New York, a distance of 3800 miles. Jed saw this as an amazing challenge, when he considered the trials and tribulations of the Boston to New York run, which was only 254 miles. Wyman's mount was a Yale California, a make unfamiliar to Jed. Photos and descriptions in The Motorcycle Magazine revealed it as simply an ordinary bicycle with a 1½ HP Yale motor clipped to the frame and driven by a whittle belt (twisted rawhide), only about ½ inch in diameter. The only modifications to the standard bicycle, other than the attached tank and battery box, were extra fork braces. He read with disbelief, and considerable envy, Part 1 of Wyman's adventures on those pages. Wyman wrote with color, and considerable literacy as follows:

Across America on a Motor Bicycle
I. Over the Sierras and Through the Snow Sheds
By George A. Wyman

Little more than three miles constituted the first day's travel of my journey across the American continent. It is just three miles from the corner of Market and Kearney streets, San Francisco, to the boat that steams to Vallejo, Cal., and, leaving the corner formed by those streets at 2:30 o'clock on the bright afternoon of May 16, less than two hours later I had passed through the Golden Gate and was in Vallejo and aboard the "ark," or houseboat, of my friends, Mr. and Mrs. Brerton, which was anchored there. I slept aboard the "ark" that night.

At 7:20 o'clock the next morning I said goodby to my hospitable hosts and to the Pacific, and turned my face toward the ocean that laps the further shore of America. I at once began to go up in the world. I knew I would go higher; also I knew my mount. I was traveling familiar ground. During the previous summer I had made the journey on a California motor bicycle to Reno, Nev., and knew that crossing the Sierras, even when helped by a motor, was not exactly a path of roses. But it was that tour, nevertheless, that fired me with desire to attempt this longer journey—to become the first motorcyclist to ride from ocean to ocean.

For thirteen miles out of Vallejo the road was a succession of land waves; one steep hill succeeded another, but the motor was working like clockwork and covered the distance in but a few moments over the hour, and in the face of a wind the force of which was constantly increasing. The further I went the harder blew the wind. Finally it actually blew the motor to a standstill. I promptly dismounted and broke off the muffler. The added power proved equal to the emergency, and the wind ceased to worry. My next dismount was rather sudden. While going well and with no thought of the road I ran full tilt into a patch of sand. I landed ungracefully, but unharmed, ten feet away. The fall, however, broke my cyclometer and also cracked the glass of the oil cup in the motor—damage which the plentiful use of the tire tape at least temporarily repaired.

Entering the splendid farming country of the Sacramento Valley, it is easy to imagine this the garden spot of the world. Magnificent farms, well kept vineyards and a profusion of peach, pear and almond orchards line the road; and that scene, so common to Californians' eyes and so odd to visitors'—great gangs of pigtailed Chinese at work with rake and hoe—is everywhere observable. At Davisville, fifty-nine miles from Vallejo, those always genial and well meaning prevaricators, the natives, informed me that the road to Sacramento, which point I had set as the day's destination, was in good shape; and though I knew that in many places the Sacramento River, swollen by the melting snow of the Sierras, had, as is the case each year, overflowed its banks, I trustingly believed them. Alas! for human faith. Eight miles from Davisville the road lost itself in the overflowing river. The water was too deep to navigate on a motor bicycle or any other bicycle, so I faced about and retraced the road for four miles, or until I reached the railroad tracks. The river and its tributaries and for several miles the lowlands are spanned by trestlework, on which the rails are laid. The crossties of the roadbed proper are not laid with punctilious exactitude, nor are the intervening spaces leveled or smoothed. They make uncomfortable and wearying walking; they make bicycle riding of any sort of dangerous when it is not absolutely impossible. On the trestles themselves the ties are laid sufficiently close together to make them ridable—rather "choppy" riding, it is true, but preferable and very much faster and less tiresome than trundling. I walked the roadbed; I "bumped it" across the trestles, and that night, the 17th, I slept in Sacramento—a day's journey of eighty-two miles—and slept soundly. It was late when I awoke, and almost noon when I left the beautiful capital of the Golden State. The Sierras and a desolate country were ahead, and I made preparations accordingly. Sacramento is but fifteen feet above sea level; the summit of the range is 7,015 feet.

Three and a half miles east of Sacramento the high trestle bridge spanning the main stream of the American River has to be crossed, and from this bridge is obtained a magnificent view of the snow capped Sierras, "the great barrier that separates the fertile valleys and glorious climate of California from the bleak and barren sage brush plains, rugged mountains and forbidding wastes of sand and alkali that, from the summit of the Sierras, stretch away to the eastward for over a thousand miles." The view from the American River bridge is imposing, encompassing the whole foothill country, which "rolls in broken, irregular billows of forest crowned hill and charming vale, upward and onward to the east, gradually growing more rugged, rocky and immense, the hills changing to mountains, the vales to canyons, until they terminate in bald, hoary peaks whose white, rugged pinnacles seem to penetrate the sky, and stand out in ghostly, shadowy outline against the azure depths of space beyond.

A few miles from Sacramento is the land of sheep. The country for miles around is a country of splendid sheep ranches, and the woolly animals and the sombreroed ranchmen are everywhere. Speeding around a bend in a road I came almost precipitately upon an immense drove which was being driven to Nevada. While the herders swore, the sheep scurried in every direction, fairly piling on top of each other in their eagerness to get out of my path. The timid, bleating creatures even wedged solidly in places. As they were headed in the same direction I was going it took some time to worry through the drove.

The pastoral aspect of the sheep country gradually gave way to a more rugged landscape, huge boulders dotting the earth and suggesting the approach to the Sierras. At Rocklin the lower foothills are encountered; the stone beneath the surface of the ground makes a firm roadbed and affords stretches of excellent going. Beyond the foothills the country is rough and steep and stony and redolent of the days of '49. It was here and hereabouts that the gold finds were made and where the rush and "gold fever" were fiercest. Desolation now rules, and only heaps of gravel, water ditches and abandoned shafts remain to give color to the marvelous narratives of the "oldest inhabitants" that remain. The steep grades also remain, and the little motor was compelled to work for its "mixture." It "chugged" like a tired and panting being up the mountains, and from Auburn to Colfax—sixty miles from Sacramento—where I halted for the night, the help of the pedals was necessary.

When I left Colfax on the morning of May 19 the motor was working grandly, and though the going was up, up, up, it carried me along without an effort for nearly ten miles. Then it overheated, and I had to "nurse" it with oil every three or four miles. It recovered itself during luncheon at Emigrants' Gap, and I prepared for the snow that had been in sight for hours and that the atmosphere told me was not now far ahead. But between the Gap and the snow there was six miles of the vilest road that mortal ever dignified by the term. Then I struck the snow, and as promptly I hurried for the shelter of the snow sheds, without which there would be no travel across continent by the northern route. The snow lies ten, fifteen and twenty feet deep on the mountain sides, and ever and anon the deep boom or muffled thud of tremendous slides of "the beautiful" as it pitches into the dark deep canyons or falls with terrific force upon the sheds conveys the grimmest suggestions.

The sheds wind around the mountain sides, their roofs built aslant that the avalanches of snow and rock hurled from above may glide harmlessly into the chasm below. Stations, section houses and all else pertaining to the railways are, or course, built in the dripping and gloomy, but friendly, shelter of these sheds, where daylight penetrates only at the short breaks where the railway tracks span a deep gulch or ravine.

To ride a motor bicycle through the sheds is impossible. I walked, of course, dragging my machine over the ties for eighteen miles by cyclometer measurement. I was seven hours in the sheds. For a brief moment, at out which there would be no travel across the road. I did not find it. It was fifteen feet under the snow. That night I slept at Summit, 7,015 feet above the sea, having ridden—or walked—fifty-four miles during the day.

The next day, May 20, promised more pleasure, or, rather, I fancied that it did so. I knew that I could go no higher, and with dark, damp, dismal snow sheds and the miles of wearying walking behind me and a long down grade before me, my fancy had painted a pleasant picture of if not smooth, then easy sailing. When I sought my motor bicycle in the morning the picture received its first blur. My can of lubricating oil was missing. The magnificent view the tip top of the mountains afforded lost its charms. I had eyes not even for Donner Lake, the "gem of the Sierras," nestling like a great, lost diamond in its setting of fleecy snow and tall, gaunt pines.

Oil such as I required was not to be had on the snowbound summit nor in the untamed country ahead, and oil I must have—or walk, and walk far. I knew that my supply was in its place just after emerging from the snowsheds the night before, and I reckoned therefore that the now prized can had dropped off in the snow, and determined to hunt for it. I trudged back a mile and half. Not an inch of ground or snow escaped search, and when at last a dark object met my gaze I fairly bounded toward it. It was my oil! I think I now know at least a thrill of the joy experienced by the traveler on the desert who discovers an unsuspected pool.

The oil, however, was not of immediate aid. It did not help me get through the dark, damp, dismal tunnel, 1,700 feet long, that afforded the only means of egress from Summit. I walked through that, of course, and emerging, continued to walk, or, rather, I tried to walk. Where the road should have been was a wide expanse of snow—deep snow. As there was nothing else to do, I plunged into it and floundered, waded, walked, slipped and slid to the head of Donner Lake. It took me an hour to cover the short distance. At the Lake the road cleared and to Truckee, 10 miles down the canyon, was in excellent condition for the season of this year. The grade drops 2,400 feet in the ten miles, and but for the intelligent Truckee citizen I would have bidden good-bye to the Golden State long before I finally did so.

The best and shortest road to Reno? The intelligent citizens, several of them agreed on the route, and I followed their directions. The result: Nearly two hours later and after riding 21 miles, I reached Bovo, six miles by rail from Truckee. After that experience I asked no further information, but sought the crossties, and although they shook me up not a little, I made fair time to Verdi, 14 miles. Verdi is the first town in Nevada and about 40 miles from the summit of the Sierras. Looking backward the snow-covered peaks are plainly visible, but one is not many miles across the State line before he realizes that California and Nevada, though they adjoin, are as unlike as regards soil, topography, climate and all else as two countries between which an ocean rolls.

Nevada is truly the "Sage Brush State." The scrubby plant marks its approach, and it front, behind, to the right, to the left, on the plains, the hills, everywhere, there is sage brush. It is almost the only evidence of vegetation, and as I left the crossties and traveled the main road the dull green of the plant had grown monotonous long before I reached Reno, once the throbbing pivot of the gold-seeking hordes attracted by the wealth of the Comstock lodes, located in themountains in the distance. That most of Reno's glory has departed did not affect my rest that night.

"1902 Yale California"

After reading this fascinating first account of Wyman's travels, Jed got out maps and did some research on the areas Wyman had covered. His imagination got the better of him as he imagined the lush vegetation and sunshine of California. "Go west, young man!" someone had said. Jed thought about it throughout the summer: if Wyman could travel east, maybe he could head west on the Orient. He began to save what little money he could.

Jed rode his Orient into Milwaukee one day in the summer of 1904. As he traveled along Howell Avenue, he spotted another motorcycle at the curb on the opposite side. It appeared to be having some problems, as the rider was making some adjustments. Jed circled in the roadway, and stopped by the other rider to see if he could render some assistance. "I'm just making a minor adjustment to the carburetion," said the young rider, a few years senior to Jed. "I think it should go better now." The machine was painted black, and had a large loop frame, with a big 3½ HP engine. "Harley Davidson" was painted on its tank.

Surprised, Jed looked at the rider with sudden recognition. "Didn't I meet you on Grand Avenue back in '96 when Pennington was demonstrating his motor cycle?"

"Yes, and you must be the kid with the milk cans," the owner of the little black bike said with a smile. "I'm Bill Harley." Bill went on to explain how he and his friend, Arthur Davidson, were experimenting with their own machine design They had been at it for a couple of years, although they felt that this machine was the first really good one. They had used a small bicycle attachment prior to this machine, but it failed to climb hills. "We hope to have our own company one day, just like those fellows Hendee and Hedstrom over in Springfield. Our plan is to build a good, reliable machine for people to use for transportation, unlike some of these other manufacturers who just seem interested in competition." Jed told Bill that he hoped to travel to the west coast on the Orient. Bill smiled and wished him well, saying that he wished he could do the same, but had to stick to his project. With that, Bill pedaled the little Harley Davidson a short distance, gave a friendly wave and putted merrily on his way.

Jed's determination to head west and make a new life for himself became stronger after his mother and Harold Wilson had exchanged vows in October of 1903. His mother moved into the "big house," with Harold and his youngest son. Then the couple decided that the Fleming house should be the new home of the oldest Wilson son and his family. The Fleming driving shed was vacated, as the black team, that had been Zeke's pride and joy, were now quartered next door, as were the buckboard and carriage. The driving shed became Jed's new quarters. Although he was close to his beloved Orient, the accommodations were neither luxurious, insulated, nor well heated. He felt rejected and abandoned by his mother, who seemed besotted by Wilson.

The winter of 1903/4 was miserable both in terms of weather and living conditions for Jed. It was cold in the shed, in spite of heat from a big old Franklin stove installed there.

Jed was served his meals in the back kitchen of "the big house" with the servants and hired hands. These became more numerous, as the increased farming operation increased in size. The only exception was the obligatory Sunday dinner with his recently extended family.

The stressful relationship between Jed and the Wilson family deteriorated over that winter. The Wilson son, who now lived in Jed's former family home, had no time for him and took to calling Jed a "lazy bastard." In one sense there was some truth in that, as Jed was rarely up in time for the beginning of the milking and occasionally failed to show up at all. Harold Wilson was not an unreasonable man entirely; he asked Jed into the parlor after one of the Sunday dinners. This meeting came about as a result of pressure put on her husband by Hanna.

"It's pretty obvious that you have very little interest in the farm, Jed," said Wilson. "You did seem to do a reasonable job of taking care of your mother's place after your father died, and we both appreciate that. It looks like you are now only interested in those noisy contraptions on two wheels that you ride, which quite frankly, I consider inventions of the devil. I would prefer not to have them on the property."

"With this in mind, and the fact that you were your father's only son and heir, prior to Hanna's and my marriage, I have set you up with a trust fund. There will be an income from it that will take care of your basic needs for ten years, at which time it will run out. By that time, I hope that you have indeed found fortune of your own. I suggest that you move into town, or wherever, as soon as it is practical, for your own piece of mind as well as for that of the rest of us."

Jed quickly signed the document provided by Harold: it revoked all claim to the former Fleming property in exchange for a letter of introduction to the Wells Fargo Bank in Milwaukee, where the trust fund had been set up. He was glad to be free of the farm. His dream was to travel west by motorcycle; he had been keenly following Wyman's west-to-east adventures and was certain he could do the same thing, but in the opposite direction.

Two days later, Jed rode his Orient into Racine, leaving his tearful mother and a rather smug looking Harold Wilson, to set up digs at his former rooming house. He could not think of anywhere else to go. The younger Wilson son followed Jed with his things in the buckboard. After he took his leave, Jed was on his own.

Jed Fleming never again returned to the farm.

CHAPTER FIVE

ALMOST SETTLING DOWN
1905 AND 1906

The day after taking his leave of the farm, Jed visited Kane's hardware, where he found immediate employment. Although motorcycles were a thing of the past there, Jed found selling hardware and sweeping the floor much less stressful than working with the Wilson clan. As a fringe benefit, unfettered access to the hoard of obsolete Orient parts in the basement allowed Jed to keep his machine in top order—in preparation for the big trip when he had accumulated sufficient funds. Between his wages and the trust fund payments, a small bank account began to grow.

"Harley Davidson Factory, 1905"

On a summer day in 1905, Jed talked Arthur Kane into visiting Bill Harley and Arthur Davidson at their premises in Milwaukee, suggesting that maybe they should take up selling these little locally made machines. They made their way in Kane's carriage. There they found Bill and Arthur working in a tiny shed, creating one machine. They had, it seemed, just recently sold one, so could start on another. At the suggestion of setting up a dealership, Bill laughed, and said, "We can sell all we can make. Until we sell the finished machine, we can't get started on the next. We don't have extra funds and certainly don't want to get into debt. That's why so many other makers of motorcycles are falling by the wayside. We don't have the money behind us those two fellows in Springfield have, either. Arthur's brother, William, wishes to join us, but we have to get ahead before he can afford to quit his job at the railroad tool room. We sure could use his help, but we can't afford the extra wages."

"Bill Harley, (right) with new model, 1905"

On the way back to the hardware store, Kane remarked to Jed, "I doubt that your two young friends are going to amount to a hill of beans. You can't get into manufacturing without good financing, and the ability to stick your neck out with the banks." Jed had to agree, although he wanted to believe that Bill and Arthur would find a way to make it work. He had a collection of brochures on various motorcycles, showing vast factories, not the least of which was that big wigwam in Milwaukee. That little shed was hardly competition, they agreed.

Events would prove them wrong—very wrong indeed.

Six months after the trip to the "shed," Arthur Kane hired a young lady to work in his office, to take care of the books, and act as secretary. A year younger than Jed, she had curly brown hair, matching brown eyes and evidence of a rather curvaceous figure under the rather severe fashions of the time. Mabel Skinner was quite the loveliest young thing Jed had ever laid eyes on. Prior to that, it had probably been a French Peugeot V-twin motorcycle that had blasted by him as he rode his Orient along the lakeshore earlier that year. He could not catch the Peugeot and, initially at least, had similar difficulty with Mabel. While Jed spent a lot of time sweeping up in Kane's office, he was unable to speak to Mabel, hindered by an inherent shyness of the only child around people his own age. When he did try to speak, he could feel his face redden and he would quickly leave, much to her amusement, as well as that of Arthur Kane.

Gradually, Jed overcame his shyness and was soon talking to Mabel whenever he could, as well as walking her home after work. She lived in a respectable lady's rooming house, not too far from his. He was, of course, permitted only to meet her in the parlor, under the watchful eyes of the landlady. Those two years, 1905 and 1906, were two of Jed's happiest; he and Mabel spent much time together, walking long distances, and spooning down by the lakeshore. Surprisingly, Jed learned that Mabel too was born on a farm, just a few concession roads from the old Fleming place. One Sunday, Mabel took Jed out to meet her parents and, as it turned out, Mr. Skinner was a Lodge Brother of Harold Wilson's. This led to an opinion of Jed that was less than complimentary. "That new boyfriend of yours is a shiftless bum," Skinner quietly mentioned to his daughter. Jed too was also uncomfortable when he saw the Skinner farm and its prized Holsteins.

Jed and Mabel took off on many expeditions the summer of 1906, mostly on foot, but occasionally with Arthur's carriage, which they were able to use now and then. Jed's motorcycle was left behind now, as there was no way of carrying a passenger. He began to see the advantage of an automobile, or at least a sidecar. They spent many evenings together on their own down by the lake.

In December, Mabel came in to the hardware store on a Monday morning and tearfully told Arthur Kane and Jed that her parents were sending her to New York to care for an aging aunt. She gave her notice and left directly afterwards. Jed rode his Orient out to the Skinner farm, where he received a frosty reception. They would not give Jed the address of the aunt. Curiously, Arthur Kane adopted a somewhat distant attitude towards Jed. Two weeks later he gave Jed a weeks pay saying he was no longer needed, as business had slowed down. This did not seem so to Jed.

Although he was not told directly what had taken place, years later he was all but certain, and had probably known it all along. Having his lover sent to visit an aunt meant the family did not think him worthy of a shotgun wedding. And perhaps he wasn't. Much as he loved Mabel, he couldn't imagine himself ending up taking care of a bunch of Holsteins again. It was not the most honorable period of his life.

Jed soon left Racine and rented rooms in Milwaukee. He kept pretty much to himself, while he planned an escape from his past. He would leave town on the bike, as soon as the snows melted.

CHAPTER SIX

FLORIDA BEACH RACING

That winter Jed was delighted to hear from his uncle George by letter. He was very tolerant of his nephew's shortcomings, probably due to the fact that he was similar in nature. George, a bit of a playboy and womanizer, could scarcely blame his nephew for being the same way. He said in the letter, "Shame on you, boy, for getting that little gal up the stump. You should be more careful. You got off lightly this time! I'm planning a train trip to Ormond Beach in January to watch motor races and speed attempts, and want you to join me. Hop the train to Boston, and we'll go together. There's a ticket enclosed. I've got a private car for us from there." Jed's past was selfishly forgotten.

On arrival in Boston, George took Jed to a tailor and had him fitted for a tuxedo. "If you are going with me, young man, you must look the part. Gentlemen dress for dinner. The private car is like a fine hotel on wheels. With our own dining room, who knows whom we will meet during our travels?"

George was now quite the railroad tycoon, and the private car was set up with all the comforts one could ask for. As they traveled to Florida, an East Indian servant in a turban pampered them with attention, keeping them plied with food and drink. It was quite a change from living in a rooming house for Jed. Train travel was pretty sophisticated in those days. In taking a walk through the other cars, Jed realized what special treatment they were receiving: there was first class, second class, third class, and way above them ranked the private car. It would be a long time before road travel ever got to this level, if ever. According to George, only ocean travel offered greater luxury than a private railroad car. "We'll get you on the Cunard Lines' Lusitania one of these days, boy. It's going to be pretty swell. She'll be making her maiden voyage later this year, sailing between New York and Liverpool." Anything more luxurious than the private rail car was quite beyond Jed's imagination.

While the two enthusiasts had a good deal to discuss and argue about on the way to Florida, making the time pass quickly. "I know you are a died-in-the-wool motorcycle enthusiast, Jed, but look at this train. It's powered by steam, as are all the great ships of the world. Anyone who wishes to get anywhere, and on time, is propelled there by steam. That's why I have a Stanley. It is smooth, quiet, and I don't have to indulge myself in that confounded twirling! Fred Marriott will be at Ormond with one of the latest *Flying Teakettles* from the Stanley brothers. The racers have 30-inch boilers, and modified 30-HP engines having better than 1:1 ratios at the rear axle. The boiler will be running on 1000 lbs of steam pressure. You are really going to see something! The previous racer, the *Wogglebug*, had twin 30 horse engines and two 24-inch boilers, but ran on more like 500 pounds. They had a tough time keeping the engines balanced with each other. That's where the name came from. The Rocket is a definite improvement."

George had a point with his love of steam power, Jed conceded, as he recalled Sylvester Roper's impressive demonstration back in 1896. "You will have a pretty interesting motorcycle to cheer for, though," said George. "That fellow Glenn Curtis from Hammondsport, New York, is showing up with a motorcycle powered by a V-8 aero engine he is developing for airships. The bloody thing is so massive, I'm sure if it starts up, it will destroy the machine and poor Glenn if he's not careful. I'm afraid Marriott will make mincemeat of him speed-wise. You can overdo a good thing!" Jed considered a minute, and then replied, "Isn't 1000 pounds of steam overdoing a good thing, when the locomotive powering this train runs on a small fraction of that?" George conceded the point with a smile.

On the second day of travel, George announced they were going to have a dinner party in the car. "Some of the racers are on the same train, Jed." To Jed's surprise, the dinner guests included Fred Marriott, Glenn Curtis, Ray Harroun, and E.B. Blakely. Blakely was to drive a 70-HP American Mercedes, while Harroun was to pilot a 468-pound lightweight car powered by his design of air-cooled V-8 airship engine. All present but Jed made rather light of Curtis's two-wheeler. Jed's money was on the two-wheeler. Curtis was very friendly towards Jed, answering all his questions, while the rest of the racers had pretty big egos. Curtis was a regular guy as far as Jed was concerned. Blakely was the only one who looked entirely at home in his evening dress and, obviously, came from money. He was a private entry in his big expensive Mercedes. Harroun was a short dark Irishman, who had entered the USA at Ellis Island ten years previously, and was now designing aero engines. Curtis had grudging admiration for Harroun's engine but thought the quadricycle it was attached to rather flimsy, and remarked on it. "I have twice as many flaming wheels as you Curtis! When you crank up your V-8, your velocipede will flip sideways!" Harroun laughed. Marriott simply smiled with the confidence of a known favorite.

While the rest of the group enjoyed their brandy and cigars, Curtis took Jed to the baggage car where the V-8 motorcycle was traveling. Along with the big machine were two more conventional Curtis motorcycles: a single and a twin, which were to be used for production-based competition at Ormond Beach. "The 8 cylinder engine displaces 244 cu. in., and is essentially four of my v-twin motorcycle engines on a common crank-case. Notice the similarity to the twin, there. The cylinders of both the twin and the 8 are set at 90 degrees, which gives ideal balance. Other manufacturers build their twin cylinder motorcycles with angles of 45 degrees, and similar. The vibration is not only unpleasant to the rider, but it can shake the machine to pieces, and leads to premature mechanical failure. The bottom end is different on the 8, obviously, and the drive is by shaft to bevel gears on the rear wheel. There is no clutch, and it is single speed. I plan to have it towed to about 40 mph, where I will drop the valve lifter, and feed the power on slowly. As you can see, the chassis is very light, so I will need to be careful so as not to break it," Glenn explained. After a few more questions from Jed, patiently answered by the kindly Curtis, Glenn made his exit, explaining he would get a good nights rest. "Let those four-wheeled people stay up and carouse. We two wheeled folks need to keep our balance. Good night, Jed."

Jed and George arrived at the beach on Thursday Jan 17, just in time to help the Stanley group repair the Rocket's streamlined shell, which had been damaged on the train ride from New England. Marriott's racer, named the "Rocket," was totally enclosed, something unseen in those days, and resembled an upturned canoe. Both the boiler and burner were located behind the driver, and, unlike conventional Stanleys, a huge exhaust flue exited aft. It was a very futuristic looking device. Jed began to feel a bit sorry for Glenn Curtis, as the Stanley was a pretty awesome device indeed. The two other Stanleys were the more conventional, proven Vanderbilt racers.

"Fred Marriot & Stanley Rocket, 1907"

The beach was very rough, and unsuitable for racing on Friday, but appeared somewhat better on Saturday. Marriott made an "unremarkable" run according to him of one mile in slightly over 38 seconds, which seemed pretty fast to George and Jed. Meanwhile Curtis bided his time, waiting for ideal conditions. Blakely's Mercedes was beaten by almost a mile in a race with one of the Vanderbilt Stanleys. Ray Harroun's machine simply collapsed in a twisted heap just after the start, when he opened the throttle of his big V-8. The frame, apparently, could not bare the strong force of the torque. With their high pressures, the Stanleys had engine breakages, caused by sudden forces. Both Vanderbilts ended up cannibalized to keep the Rocket going.

The most spectacular day in Stanley history occurred on Friday Jan 30th, the last day of beach racing in 1907. The pressure on the Rocket was increased to 1300 pounds by cranking down the steam automatic valve. Marriott decided to go for it. With 1300 pounds on tap, he had to be very careful, as two engines had been wrecked already due to the pressure of 1000 pounds. Opening the throttle too quickly would bend the connecting rods. The throttle valve needed to be opened slowly, not only to save engine damage on startup, but also to conserve maximum pressure for the measured mile. He did a mile in 32 seconds flat, and then returned for a run of 29-3/5 seconds. Like Roper's steam cycle back in 1896, the Rocket did its runs in almost total silence. Marriott then tried again, and was traveling even faster, when the front end become airborne. The car flipped on to its side, smashing against the track with pieces scattering for two miles along the beach. The 30-inch boiler spun through the surf making a remarkable sight with steam spewing from its fractured header pipe like a giant July 4th pinwheel. Remarkably, Marriott survived to tell the tale.

George and Jed rushed over to the scene of the crash to see Marriott, rendered senseless, lying on his back in the sand with one of his eyeballs literally popped from his head. "I'm a doctor!" hollered a man breaking through the gathering crowd. Quickly surveying the situation, the doctor gently took Marriott's eye and slid it back into its socket, where it popped in with slurping noise. Jed felt weak at the knees and had to sit down. George simply passed out. Fred Marriott was quoted many years later praising that anonymous doctor and saying the sight in that particular eye was far superior to his other.

The Rocket's best time had been a mile in 29-3/5 seconds, or 121.6 mph. George had his stopwatch on the last run. Like the local press, he estimated Marriott was doing 150 mph when the Rocket flipped and crashed. Placing the heavy boiler in the rear to add traction, had made the Rocket's front end too light, and the streamlined body had given it lift, not unlike an aircraft, according to Glenn Curtis, who had watched the runs with George and Jed.

Even Jed had to admit that compared to the Stanley's spectacular explosion, Glenn Curtis's effort seemed a bit anticlimactic. The V-8 motorcycle was towed to 40mph by an automobile, at which point Curtis dropped the valve lifter, fed on the power, and passed the car as if it were standing still. The roar of the V-8 was far different from the silence of the Rocket. Curtis sped across the measured mile in 26-2/5 seconds—faster than the last measured mile by the Rocket. This speed of 136.36 mph made Glenn the fastest man in the world. Unfortunately, there were arguments that were never resolved, as the drive on the bike gave out on the return run, so no "official" record was made. The universal joint, a flimsy affair, had broken just as Curtis turned on the power to pass the towing vehicle on his second run. As he later explained to Jed, he designed it in such a way that it was the weakest link. "Better to break that part, than allow the frame to twist, or to have the hub spin out from the rear wheel. I'd rather not kill myself, as I have lots to do in my life." How right he was. Needless to say, George and Jed argued the entire way back to Boston over who was the fastest human being, Marriott or Curtis. Nevertheless one thing was certain: history had established a marker; it would be several years before a car would agian travel as quickly as had the Stanley Rocket, or a motorcycle as quickly as Glenn Curtis's V-8.

"Glen Curtis with V-8, 1907"

Jed returned to the relative obscurity of his Milwaukee rooming house, where he began to plan his own adventure, a trip across the continent following the route taken by George Wyman in 1903.

CHAPTER SEVEN

PLANNING THE CROSS-AMERICA RIDE; THE WYMAN EXAMPLE

Jed came to realize that the key to George Wyman's success in crossing the country was in following rail lines, as this afforded the most direct route. Wyman spent many miles of his fifty-one day expedition riding on the railway ties. Remarkably, the little Yale California he rode had got Wyman to New York on July 6 1903 in rather good condition, although the engine had given up, and he was forced to pedal the last 150 miles. As Jed re-read Wyman's last article, he considered the great challenge he was facing, hoping he was up to the task.

Motorcycle Magazine: The last leg: Chicago to New York, Date

With the Windy City at my back, I felt as if I would "blowin" to New York in a week or so. The worst roads I knew must surely be behind me, and, with better highways, I calculated that I would have no more trouble with my motor bicycle. I reckoned without thought of the cumulative effects of the continuous battering that the machine was receiving. It had proven itself a wonderfully staunch steed, but no vehicle could stand what I imposed upon this ninety pound vehicle, nor should any be expected to do so. Before I got through with my trip I had, as will be seen, a vivid personal experience that put me into thorough sympathy with the Deacon and his one horse shay.

As I have said, I did not want to remain in Chicago one minute longer than was necessary, and accordingly I left there at 5:30 p.m., on June 23, and made my way to Kensington, twenty-three miles east. In the morning I ordered and paid for some gasoline. What I got was a vile mixture of gasoline and something that was much like linseed oil. I believe it was that, but I did not discover the imposition until after I had started, and I did not go back. A man who will sell such stuff has no conscience. Only a club will appeal to him, and I had no time to waste in fighting. I simply went on and made the best of it till I could get fresh gasoline elsewhere. The roads were heavy from recent rains when I left Kensington at 6:45 a.m., and here in the smooth and "built up" east I had to resort to the trick I learned in the deserts of Nevada and Utah. I took to the railroad track, and rode twenty miles along the ties to the lake. I saved a considerable distance by following the railroad, and as I was seasoned to such riding, the bouncing did not hurt so much as did the thought that I was having the same sort of traveling east of Chicago that I had west of Omaha. Well, it is a big country to build up and supply with good roads. Any one who has made such a trip as I made can appreciate this in a fullness that others cannot. When this country is eventually built up with good roads it will be truly great and wonderful.

I left the railroad at Porter, Indiana, and got on to a road with a good rock bed, which lasted for several miles. The rains, which had so severely damaged the roads, had not hurt the crops much, so far as I could see. It was all a "ranching country," as we say in the West—farming they call it in the East—through which I was passing at this stage, and itlooked flourishing. I reached La Porte at noon, and lunched there, having made 55 miles in the forenoon. I had been keeping company with a smell like that of burning paint all the morning. It came from the mixture that I was exploding in the motor. I got fresh gasoline at La Porte, and at least had an honest smell for my money after that. I passed through Goshen at 5 p.m., and reached Ligonier, where I stopped for the night at 6:30 p.m. The roads began to get better after I left La Porte, and the last nineteen miles of this day's run were made in an hour and ten minutes.

I thought that when I got east of Chicago folks would know what a motor bicycle is, but it was not so. In every place through which I passed I left behind a gaping lot of natives, who ran out into the street to stare at me. When I reached Ligonier I rode through the main street, and by mistake went past the hotel where I wanted to stop. When I turned and rode back the streets looked as though there was a circus in town. All the shopkeepers were out on the sidewalks to see the motor bicycle, and small boys were as thick as flies in a country restaurant. When I dismounted in front of the hotel, the crowd became so big and the curiosity so great that I deemed it best to take the bicycle inside. The boys manifested a desire to pull it apart to see how it was made. There was really more curiosity about my motor bicycle in the eastern towns than in the wilds of the Sierras. The mountaineers are surprised at nothing, and seemed to have caught from the Indians the self-containment that disdains to manifest the slightest curiosity. Although, when spoken to about it, the Westerners would frankly admit they never saw such a machine before, yet they turned toward me on my first appearance the same stolid countenances with which they gazed at the sky and the surrounding landscape. This day, when I reached Ligonier, June 24, I had made 130 miles.

At 8 a.m. on June 25 I left Ligonier and struck out over a sandy road, through a rolling and fertile farming country, to Wawaka, where I came to a stone road, and had good riding to Kendalville. East of that place, to Butler, the going was a good second to what I had in Iowa, which was the worst of anywhere that there were roads. Between Butler and Edgerton, after having ridden 48 miles from Ligonier, I crossed the State line into Ohio. The road improved some then, but was very bad in places all the way to Swanton, at which place I resorted to the railroad for more comfort and fewer dismounts. I rode nine miles to Holland along the tracks, but the railroad bed was a poor one and about as rough riding as the road, so I returned to the highway and found a six-mile stretch of good road south to Miami. By taking this road I made a short cut that saved me fifteen miles, and did not, therefore, see Toledo. I arrived at Perryburg, Ohio at 7 p.m., with 126 miles to my credit for the day. The price of gasoline continued to decrease as I got farther East. In the morning of that day at Ligonier I had paid ten cents for half a gallon; at Butler I got the same quantity for eight cents, and at Swanton the price was seven cents. The table board did not improve, however. For me, with my vigorous Western appetite, the bounteous supply of plain food served by the little hotels in the Rocky Mountain country was much more satisfactory than anything I got in the East. The meals out in Nevada and Wyoming were much better than anything I got in Illinois, Indiana or Ohio, at the same price. Everywhere I stopped during this part of my trip a crowd gathered about me and my motorcycle, although neither the machine nor myself had on any sign telling our mission. Whenever I told someone in a crowd I had come from San Francisco there was at first open incredulity. The word was passed along, and they winked to one another, while staring impudently at me. At this stage of my journey I had with me, however, a copy of the June issue of *The Motorcycle Magazine*, with the story of my start from the Coast and a picture. This convinced the doubters, and immediately my bicycle became an object of unbounded curiosity, while I was the target for a Gatling-gun fire of questions that was impossible to answer satisfactorily. The consequence was I became more particular when and where I took the trouble to convince people of my feat. About this time I began to feel the effects of my five days' rest in Chicago. That length of time led to my growing tender, and I was more saddle-sore at Perrysburg that night than at any time before. I felt then as if I would have to finish with a hot water bag on the saddle. From Perrysburg I got a 7 o'clock start, but soon discovered that I did not have any more lubricating oil than enough to last for thirty miles. By economizing I managed to reach Fremont where I got some oil at a machine shop. It was so thick that I had to heat it before it would run but it was better than nothing. After leaving Fremont the roads began to grow very poor. There had been several days of rain on them just before I came along and as they were simply dirt roads for repeated stretches of ten miles or more the mud was deep and wide.

Near Amherst about thirty miles west of Cleveland I got my first reminder of the one-horse story and a foretaste of what was in store for me. The truss on the front forks of my bicycle broke, and when I stopped to remove the remains of it, I found that it had crystallized so that is was like a piece of old rusty iron. It broke in several places like a stick of rotten wood. That was the effect of the terrible pounding the machine had received over the railroad ties. It occurred to me at the time that the whole machine must have suffered similarly, but it did not show signs of disintegrating at the time, and I concluded it would carry me to New York. After leaving Elyria, twenty-five miles from Cleveland, I struck a good side path that continued for twenty miles. It was only six inches wide in places, but those few inches spelled salvation for me, because the road was so heavy with sand that I had not had the path to ride I would have had to walk for long stretches. Just out of Elyria I met an automobile, and it was having a hard time of it. It was all the engine could do to keep it moving. The last five miles into Cleveland I went over the best roads I ever had ridden on anywhere in my life.

It was 7 p.m. when I reached Cleveland, and my first move was to hunt up an automobile station in order to get some oil. At the Oldsmobile branch I found what I wanted, and they gave me enough to last for three hundred miles, all I cared to carry, in fact. They took a lively interest in me and my bicycle and examined my motor carefully. Like every one else though, they had to be shown the photographs of my start from San Francisco before fully accepting my statement that I had come from California. My distance for this day, to Cleveland, was 121 miles, and I used five quarts of gasoline.

It was on the day I left Cleveland, June 27, when my troubles began to come thick and fast. I started from Cleveland at 10 a.m. and had gone only a mile when the lacing holes in my driving belt gave way and I had to stop and replace. For the first five miles the road was fine, and then I came to a stretch where the road was being rebuilt and I had to walk for a mile and a half. After that I had a plank road for six miles, all the way to Geneva. From there to Conneaut, twenty-two miles, the road was good in places, with occasional stretches of clay and sand, through which it was hard going. It was a dreary day of travel through a pretty farming country, where the ranchers seemed to be as heavy-witted as the cattle. The belt broke five times during the afternoon, and the last time I fixed it I laced it with two inches of space between the ends in order to make it reach. I passed through town after town, where I wondered what the people did for recreation. There was nothing for them to do after their day's work but to walk around the block and then go to bed. One thing I noticed is that it is a poor country for shoemakers for nearly everyone I saw, men, women and children, were barefooted. It was plain that much of the country I saw was settled by immigrant farmers from Germany and other parts of Europe. I made only seventy-five miles this day. When I arrived at Conneaut, I got a piece of belting at a bicycle store and spliced my troublesome piece of driving leather. Then I discovered that the screws in the crank case of the motor were all loose, so I put in some white lead and tightened them. It was so late by this time that I concluded to remain at Conneaut over night. My hoodoo was with me all the next day. I left Conneaut at 7:30 a.m., and before I had gone quite ten miles the oil began to leak out of the crank case, although I had done my best to make it tight and seal it with white lead the night before. The belt again gave out and I had my own profane troubles with these two defects all day. First it was the oil, and then the belt, and I became so disgusted before noon that I felt like shooting the whole machine full of holes and deserting it. This was my first visit to Pennsylvania—for I had been riding in the little fifty mile strip of the Keystone State that borders on Lake Erie ever since leaving Conneaut—and I can say that all my Pennsylvania experiences were hard ones. The roads were fairly good and for most of the way. I rode on footpaths at the side of the road. The view from the road with the luxuriant verdure clad bluffs on one side and the horizon-bounded expanse of the great lake on the other side was as magnificent as I had seen. It reminded me of the good old Pacific.

By afternoon I had crossed the Pennsylvania strip and was at last in New York State. It seemed as if I was nearing home then, but it is a big State, and I came to realize the truth of the song that "it's a blanked long walk to the gay Rialto in New York." I didn't have to walk, but walking would have been easier than the way I traveled from the western boundary of the Empire State to the metropolis. It was on the afternoon of June 28 that I entered the State, and it was eight days later before I got to the confines of the great city. I had hoped to reach Buffalo on the day I left Conneaut, but I was still twenty-five miles from the Queen City when my troubles climaxed by the breaking of a forkside. The crystallization resulting from the continuous pounding was telling again. I walked two miles into Angola, and there sought a telegraph office, and wired Chicago for a pair of new forks. I learned that I would not be able to get a pair there for two days, because they would have to go first to Buffalo and then be reshipped to Angola. I therefore determined to get the forks repaired there if possible, and make them do till I got to Buffalo. It is a fortunate thing that I was not riding fast or going down hill when the forkside broke. I was told that automobiles and motor bicycles frequently traveled the road that I took from Chicago to New York, but the behavior of the natives belied it. The people all came running out of the houses when I passed, and they stared as if they never had seen a motor bicycle before.

I spent two hours in a repair shop in Angola the next morning, June 29, and at the end of that time the repairer pronounced the forks mended sufficiently to carry me through to New York. I did not feel as confident about this as the repairman did. I got to Buffalo by 11 o'clock, and after a visit to the post office, I rode out to the E. R. Thomas automobile and motor bicycle factory. There I met Mr. E.

R. Thomas for the first time, and I must pay a tribute to his generous hospitality, which I shall always remember. His kindness was all the more magnanimous when it is remembered that I was riding the product of a rival maker. The first thing Mr. Thomas did was to send my bicycle inside and have it seen to that it was supplied with oil and gasoline. Then he learned that my forks were in bad shape, and he ordered men to get to work and make a new pair for it and finish them at night. The men worked in the factory until 9 o'clock that night on my forks, and had them ready for me to make an early start in the morning. For all this Mr. Thomas would not accept payment. In the meantime he showed me through his factory, and then lent me an Auto-Bi, on which I took a trip about the city.

"I left Buffalo at 5:20 a.m., determined, if possible, to get to New York by July 2, and join in the endurance run to Worcester that started on the third. After I had gone ten miles the lacing holes in the belt broke away again. I then put on the old original belt with which I had started from San Francisco and which I removed at Chicago, but still carried with me. Everything went finely for the next few miles, and then the connecting rod of the motor broke.

Everything seemed to me to be going to pieces. There was nothing for it then but to pedal, and I churned away for five miles into Batavia. It was only 9 a.m. when I got there, and it took until 3:30 p.m. to get the repairs made so that I could start again. It went all right until I was twelve miles from Rochester, and then the valves got to working so poorly that I could not make more than five miles an hour with it. I managed to reach a cycle store in Rochester, and there I went to work, intending to get it fixed and ride half the night to make up for lost time. It was of no use. I worked until 11 p.m., and then gave it up until morning. I realized then that the motor and bicycle were suffering from crystallization. There were no flaws or defects of any sort in the parts that were breaking. They were just giving out all at once, like the Deacon's famous shay that served him so well and so long and was not weaker in any one part than in another. In spite of all my troubles, I had made eighty miles that day, and I still had hopes of being in New York in time for the fireworks. It took until 11:30 o'clock the next day, July 1, to get the motor working, and then I started from Rochester with G. D. Green, superintendent of the Regas Company, and W. L. Stoneburn, the bookkeeper, riding with me as an escort. They accompanied me ten miles to Fairport, over roads so muddy as to be nearly impassable. Not far from Fairport, when I was alone again, the hoodoo asserted itself. First the connecting rod worked loose, and soon after the belt ends gave way. I lost as little time as possible, however, and at night I reached Cayuga, and the satisfaction of having covered seventy miles during the short day.

I left Cayuga at 8 a.m. and took my troubles with me. The batteries were growing weak; first the eyelets of the belt broke, and then the lacing; next the crank axle got out of true, and every time it struck the belt broke. I had these troubles all day. Toward night the belt broke five times in one mile. I got some new batteries at Syracuse, but after going two miles on them they would not yield a spark, so I went back and returned them, and after a search I managed to get some good batteries. The fates seemed in a conspiracy to prevent me getting to New York before July 4. The motor was getting in such shape that I realized I would be lucky if I could finish with it at all. To add to my troubles these two days from Rochester, July 1 and 2, were terribly hot and I was nearly prostrated by the heat. I managed to make sixty-five miles, and get to Canastota by 9:30 p.m. on the 2nd, and as that was the day I had hoped to be in the metropolis, I did not go to bed in any cheerful humor. At 7 a.m. on July 3, I started from Canastota, determined to get to Albany, at least, that day. I had trouble from the start. I replaced the belt seven times during the forenoon, and then I spliced it with a new piece at Little Falls. I was still forty miles from Albany when my handlebars broke off on one side. I had been there a couple of times before during the trip, and it did not take me long to lash a stick across the steering stem. Soon after the piston began to squeak, and I discovered that the rings on it were worn out. Oil was of no avail, and I rode on with the squeak for company. Six miles from Albany, while I was on the towpath, the rear tire blew out. There was a hole in it that would admit a hand. I walked into Albany. Some of the remarks I made to myself as I walked were not fit for quoting to a Sunday school class. My distance that day was 135 miles. This was to be my last day of big mileage though. All the way through New York State I used the cycle path without a license. It was not until after my trip ended that I knew I had been violating the law.

On the Fourth of July my first move in the morning was to a bicycle store, where I got a new tire and put in fourteen new spokes, and then took the motor apart. The piston rings were pretty thin, but looked as if they would still give service, so at 2:30 p.m. I started from Albany. Four miles out, I gave it up. The motor would not explode as it should. I went back to the bicycle store in Albany and worked on the problem there until night. Then I went to see the fireworks and forget about it. As I could not make the motor work, I concluded on the morning of July 5 to make myself work. I started to pedal in to New York. That last 150 miles down the Hudson from Albany is a part of my trip of which I will always have a vivid recollection. I had seen some hills before, but the motor climbed them for me. The hills along the Hudson I had to climb and push the motor along. They seemed steeper than the Rocky Mountains. This I will say, though—from the time I left the Pacific Coast I saw no grander scenery than that along the Hudson River. While other sights were not up to expectation, the scenery of the Hudson was far beyond it.

So enthusiastic was I that I pedaled along all night on July 5. It was a long, dreary and strenuous ride, but I was well seasoned by this time and fit to do a mule's work. After riding two days and a night under leg power or rather over it

I reached New York in the middle of the afternoon on July 6. I made frequent stops to rest and I attracted more than a little attention but I was too tired to care. I can smile now as I recall the sight I was with my overalls on, my face and hands black as a mulatto's, my coat torn and dirty, a big piece of wood tied on with rope where my handlebars should be, and the belt hanging loose from the crankshaft. I was told that I was "picturesque" by a country reporter named "Josh," who captured me for an interview a little way up the Hudson, and who kept me talking while the photographer worked his camera, but to my idea I was too dirty to be picturesque. At any rate, I was too tired then to care. All I wanted was a hot bath and a bed, but before I got these I had to telephone to the *Motorcycle Magazine* to learn where to go and wait to have more cameras pointed at me before being escorted to my hostelry. Of all the sleeps I had during my trip, none was more profound, or sweeter than the one I had that night of July 6 at the Herald Square Hotel, just fifty days after I left San Francisco for my ride across the continent on my motor bicycle.

While I slept at the Herald Square Hotel, my ride really ended at the New York Motor Cycle Club's rooms, No. 1904 Broadway. It was there I left the faithful little machine that had carried me some 3,800 miles. What was the exact distance I never will be able to tell because, as previously related, after breaking four cyclometers I ceased to bother with the mileage.

Compared with the first cycling journey across the continent, that of Thomas Stevens in 1882, the first effort of the motor bicycle does not suffer. Mr. Stevens required 103 1/2 days to ride from San Francisco to Boston; my journey was completed in 50 days. While the idea of establishing a record was no part of my purpose, it is worthy of remark that none of the three powerful automobiles that have since crossed the continent have come near to equaling my time. With the experience gained and with a more powerful machine—the one I used was of but 1 1/4 horsepower—I feel confident that the journey from ocean to ocean can be made in 30 days without particularly strenuous effort. With a railway attachment, such as in common use by bicyclists in the West, and which would permit the use of rails across the deserts of Nevada, it will be possible to more than realize the 30 days' estimate.

While it is true that my forks broke and the motor crank axle also gave way, these are unusual accidents; nearly all of my other troubles were minor ones, the belt being a most prolific source. But, as a whole, the motor behaved splendidly and performed its work well under many trying conditions. Its failure at Albany was really the only occasion when it gave me serious concern. Subsequent examination proved that the inlet valve had in some way become jammed so as to be immovable, at least with the means at my command. Between fear of breaking something and anxiety to reach New York, I possibly did not take the chances at making a strenuous repair that under other circumstances I would have taken. Save the forks, the bicycle also stood up well. The wonder is that it stood up at all so terrific and so frequent was the pounding it received in the many miles of cross-tie travel. The saddle, too, deserves praise. Despite its many drenchings and mud and snow and the heat of the desert and the banging of the railroad ties, it did not stretch or sag the fractional part of an inch, and reached New York in as good condition as when it left San Francisco.

After having read this detailed account of Wyman's several times, Jed concluded that tough as it appeared to be, he could do the trip. His 3½ HP Orient, with its engine developed by no less a personage than Oscar Hedstrom, was rather obsolete now, compared to newer machines he saw from time to time. The newer bikes were lower with fenders to protect the riders from mud. Additionally, they had more horsepower and even had sprung forks, which would certainly smooth out those rough roads, as well as the railroad ties which he knew he would be forced to travel on where there were no roads. He decided he needed a newer bike. To this end, he wrote his uncle George, and secured a loan.

He was very tempted by the new Indian, but then there was the manufacturer right there in Milwaukee. The little shed had now been supplemented by another brick building, and Bill Harley and Arthur Davidson were manufacturing as many machines as they could within the confines of their very conservative approach to building a business. They were to produce 200 during the two years of 1906, and 1907. The Harley looked like a tough little machine, so Jed ordered one for spring delivery. He was able to visit and actually see his machine being built. The Harley cost $210.00 and came with a carrier Bill Harley fitted for him at no extra cost as favor, a necessity for the upcoming adventure. He had it finished in Renault Gray, rather than black. It was extremely well finished with a polished aluminum crankcase, (Indian painted theirs), and the whole machine had the look of something lovingly assembled. This was understandable, as the bike was all hand built by Bill and Arthur. When he rode it away from the Harley Davidson plant, he couldn't believe the difference. This was a truly modern machine. He found a young customer for his old Orient, and pocketed $75.00, before watching it disappear down the road. It was his last link to his past.

What he forgot in his planning, was that Wyman had pedaled, pushed and dragged his 90-pound machine a good many miles; the Harley weighed almost twice that. Wyman also had a magazine and a manufacturer supporting him, whereas Jed had only his own resources, and his uncle George, who still doted on him. Good railway connections were available through George as well, as he was now a major shareholder in more than one. Jed even had a railroad travel pass. Four years had passed since Wyman's trip, so hopefully some new roads had been built in the meantime.

Jed decided, wisely, to retrace Wyman's route. He was saving a few miles, as he wasn't going from coast to coast, but from Milwaukee, but his thinking was that if San Francisco was warm, Los Angeles must be warmer, as it was farther south. He decided to end his trip there. He had enjoyed the Florida sunshine and hoped for a similar climate in California. Los Angeles would add about three hundred and fifty miles, or thereabouts, so the total distance would be close to Wyman's. He wanted to get to a warm climate after freezing his ass off in Wisconsin winters. Also, he wished to break away from life as it was at this point, which he realized he had really screwed up. Memories of Mabel haunted him in between dreams of motorbikes and the adventure ahead.

CHAPTER EIGHT

JED FLEMING KICKS OFF HIS CROSS-AMERICA RIDE

On the clear morning of May 10, 1907, Jed pushed the little Harley Davidson out from behind the rooming house, pedaling away just after sunup. He owed a couple of weeks back rent, and irresponsibly figured that the unneeded items he left behind would compensate the landlady. What she would do with threadbare men's clothing and a pair of broken De Dion crankcases was anybody's guess. He had packed his worthwhile belongings, including his tuxedo, in a trunk that he had stored at the railroad station awaiting his forwarding address when he reached his new home and life in California.

Bill Harley was the only person aware of Jed's plans, besides his uncle George in Boston. Bill Harley and Jed had both wished one another well in their endeavors. One would fare far better than the other. Jed had a Gladstone bag strapped to the carrier, and a canvas rucksack over his shoulder. He carried a few essential spares, clothes, of course, and he also carried a 32 cal. revolver. The gun was small compared to the "hog's legs" he would see on the cowboys he would no doubt meet, but it was light and, he hoped, would be a deterrent in case of trouble. Jed also carried enough cash to make it to the next Wells Fargo Bank. He was clever enough not to carry too much at any one time, which would stand him in good stead later. His spirits were up for the first time in months.

He motored straight south to Chicago, where he would intersect the route taken by Wyman. It was a relatively short 92 miles. The road was good graded gravel, and he had made good time. The Harley Davidson had proven to be a great mount. After checking into a hotel, Jed decided to see the sights. George Wyman had hated Chicago, as it was a wild place; he was disgusted with the many drunken men and women he had seen on the streets. Wyman also added that he didn't drink, smoke, or chew, whereas Jed had experimented with all three and had no such hang-ups. As he wandered about the downtown streets, he witnessed the partying described by Wyman, and decided to see what it was all about. He wandered into a saloon, and soon was part of the scene.

The following morning, Jed awoke with a headache and little memory of how he got to his hotel room. He turned and saw an older woman snoring in his bed, who looked as bad as he felt. Through waves of nausea, he remembered sneaking her up the back stairway the night before, when she had looked much better to him. He arose, quickly dressed, grabbed his gear, and quietly made his exit, without awakening his companion. He headed west out of town and stopped for breakfast at a hotel about a mile away. He soon regained his composure, and reflected on his evening, realizing that he had better be more careful in the future, or he would never make it to California. Fortunately, he still had his stash of cash.

After a light breakfast, and several cups of coffee to restore his well being, he pedaled off; the little Harley instantly started, and he motored towards Dixon on the old stage road. The road was rough, but the spring forks on the Harley Davidson smoothed out those bumps quite well. Additionally, the 28x2½ tires on the bike were an improvement over the old Orient's 28x2's for absorbing road shocks. By one o'clock that day, Jed was in Dixon, where he enjoyed a sizable lunch of steak and eggs. The fresh air and the open road had cleared the cobwebs and guilt over the debauchery of the night before in the Windy City.

After filling the Harley with gasoline, Jed took off, crossing the Rock River just past Nelson on the railway trestle. The ties were fairly close together on the trestle, so the ride was not too rough. He passed through Sterling, following the railroad line towards Clinton, Iowa. To reach Clinton, he needed to cross the mighty Mississippi. Rather than taking the trestle again, he decided to take the roadway down to the bank and cross on the small stern-wheeled ferry he could see just pulling in on his side of the river.

The boatmen were very curious about his motorcycle and peppered him with questions, after insisting that he shut it down to push on and off, due to the presence of the other vehicles, all of which were horse drawn. These rural horses were exceedingly skittish near any motor vehicle, and motorcycles seemed to affect them worse than any other type. Jed propped his bike by the rail, enjoying the crossing, which was all that more interesting because of the close passing of a huge passenger sternwheeler. As he exchanged waves with the well-dressed people lining its rail, he thought of the riverboat gamblers and other characters he had read about that plied this river. Two cargo steamers also passed, one heading north with cotton bales on its deck, then another with crates of cargo and two new traction engines heading south. This was America's major highway in 1907. Upon reaching the west bank, Jed started the Harley, and with some LPA (light pedal assistance), was soon up the hill and into the center of Clinton Iowa, where he found a hotel room, had dinner and a very quiet evening.

Early the next morning, Jed looked outside and saw that it was raining heavily. After a good breakfast, he loaded up the carrier, threw his satchel over his shoulder and was off again down the road, this time with Marshalltown Iowa his planned destination. The first 90 miles was hell, apart from the good lunch he had in Cedar Rapids. The fenders certainly kept the mud from plastering him as was the case with the fender-less Orient. Nevertheless another problem presented itself when the sticky mud jammed up under the fenders, slowing him down. He made frequent stops to remove the mud with the assistance of a stick he picked up along the way for this purpose. Also, when the rain stopped, and the mud was still present, the engine began to run hot as the cooling fins filled with mud as well. He picked up a smaller stick to clear the fins. Gradually the mud gave way to rutted hard clay, which gave a rougher but faster ride. There were cornfields on both sides of the roadway throughout most of the day's ride. It was not a bad day considering the weather. He'd only crashed twice and the mud had provided a soft landing for him and the Harley. Jed reached Marshalltown just as dusk was settling in, aided by a full moon, where he found a Chinese laundry that was open late. When he took his muddy clothes inside, the owner jabbered away in an unfamiliar strange language, obviously upset with the mud, but took Jed's money anyway. The clothes were ready for him the following morning, after a leisurely breakfast at a rather nice hotel.

After a few minor mechanical adjustments, Jed easily pedaled off, continuing along the road towards Ames. Barely out of town, he came across a pair of elderly ladies driving a carriage traveling in the opposite direction. As he approached, the horse became very frightened and began to buck out of control, threatening to capsize the vehicle. Jed stopped and, after leaning the Harley against a tree, ran back to render assistance. He grabbed the horse's halter; on doing so, the horse became even more agitated and would have trampled him had he not been quick on his feet. The lady handling the reins jumped down from the carriage, pushed Jed roughly aside, and calmed the frightened animal. "You!" she thundered at him, "stand thee there, and do not move. Do not dare start that devilish machine until we are well out of sight. If God intended man to ride mechanical horses, He would have provided them." With that, after re-seated herself in the carriage beside her companion, she proceeded east without a wave or backward look at the astonished motorcyclist. Jed recalled reading that George Wyman had a similar experience not too far from there during his 1903 expedition. Could these two ladies be the same ones? Stranger things have happened, he reflected.

Jed had an early light lunch at a hotel in Ames, before carrying on to Denison, arriving at dusk. He was very pleased with the Harley Davidson so far. The only problem he found was the rather flimsy throttle control linkage from the handlebar, which he had to repair once already. The simple lever controls he had had on the Orient made more sense to Jed. That problem proved to be rather minor, however. He fielded the usual questions from the locals over a cold beer in the railroad hotel. For the most part, they told Jed he was crazy to be attempting such a trip. Only about half of them even believed he had come as far as he had.

As morning dawned as another sunny day, Jed was able to take to the road again and, although it was badly rutted and rough, he decided that it was a better choice than the Northwestern Railroad, which was not too far off just in case he needed to take to the rails. It was rumored at the time, that as no one had heard from George Wyman since his crossing of the continent, that he may have succumbed to internal injuries sustained while riding the railroad ties. Jed figured that roads, when available, were a better option. While weather could make the roads impassable, he was not out to prove anything and could afford time to wait out any meteorological unpleasantness.

The road was very rough for the forty miles towards Woodbine, where Jed stopped to tighten various fasteners, top-up the gasoline and oil and find a mid-day meal. By afternoon Jed reached Council Bluffs, and the railway trestle crossing the Missouri River to Omaha, Nebraska, where he decided on an early stop. He wandered the town and marveled at its streets, which were paved in vitrified brick. He rode up and down the main street a few times, relishing in its comparative smoothness. "Ah, if only all the roads were like this," he reflected. He was enjoying himself and decided to celebrate his well being with a whiskey and a couple of beers at an inviting saloon. He was a little more careful here than in Chicago, and enjoyed a good night's rest afterwards.

At 8:40 the next morning, Jed was back on the Harley, heading west on a pretty decent dirt road. With a slight breeze at his back, and the sun shining down on him, he was a happy traveler. For the first time since his trip began, he had no thoughts of home, family, or Mabel. That was all left behind him in the dust cloud.

The little bike puttered along merrily, without missing a beat. Jed stopped at the railroad hotel in Fremont to enjoy a good noon meal of liver and onions along with a cold beer. He arrived in Columbus Nebraska at three-thirty in the afternoon, where he decided to stop for a few adjustments. After securing a room at the hotel, Jed spent the rest of the daylight hours tinkering with the bike. A few loose spokes needed attention, then a quick valve adjustment and cleaning of the carburetor and spark plug. While he was attending to these tasks, the usual group of young men and boys gathered about to admire the bike and ask questions. Some were amazed at his progress so far, although it was beyond comprehension for most, as nearly all of them had never been beyond 25 miles of Columbus.

Heading west from Columbus the following morning, Jed noticed a marked difference, as the roads were decidedly worse. He decided to take to the railroad line, which was a considerable improvement. The roadbed was sandy, almost covering the ties. Jed passed through Central City in 3½ hours; he carried on through Chapman to Grand Island, where he had a noon meal. Shortly after this, as he continued on the railroad, he rounded a corner where he faced an approaching train. He stopped the bike and jumped off the tracks with it. With the machine he tumbled down a steep embankment and into some swampy water. By the time he made it out of his predicament, he had almost been eaten alive by mosquitoes. As he made his escape from a following swarm, he decided that the roads, rough, muddy or not, were a safer bet. At a near crossing, Jed took to the dirt road once again, reaching Kearney as the sun was setting. He had covered 108 miles for the day—not too bad considering the struggle in and out of the swamp. A bit of saloon time was in order.

After a relaxed breakfast the following day, Jed headed west again and towards Lexington, where he looked up J.S. Bancroft, who had helped Wyman on his trip four years earlier. Bancroft had an excellent bicycle and automobile repair station; he gave Jed the run of the place for adjustments and repairs. He was able to pick up supplies, such as extra batteries and a couple of fresh spark plugs. Bancroft no longer had the Columbia motorcycle he'd owned on Wyman's visit. He had replaced it with a new *Indian Twin*, the first Jed had laid eyes on. Bancroft rode about ten miles west from Lexington with Jed, before turning back, after wishing him well on his ambitious ride.

Riding beside Bancroft, Jed realized that that extra cylinder made quite a difference. He vowed his next machine would be a twin. He loved the offbeat sound of the little Indian as it cruised beside him, easily pulling ahead when the throttle was opened. The Harley single continued to run steadily though, getting Jed safely to Maxwell for the evening. Maxwell was a small place, and Jed was given a room with three beds: one occupied by a railroad surveyor in one, a peddler in the second, Jed took the third. Sometimes travelers had to share a bed in smaller hotels.

The following day it was raining heavily. Jed pushed on regardless, as he had no desire to spend another night in Maxwell with his snoring companions. Shortly out of town it was raining so hard he got off the bike and simply pushed it for a couple of miles through the sticky gumbo. When the rain lightened up slightly, he fired up again, and skidded and slithered his way through North Platte and on to Paxton. Here Jed had a meal while he waited out the rain was for a couple of hours. After a damp afternoon, Jed reached Ogallala in the evening. Ogallala was another tiny place; offering only another shared room for the night. Fortunately, the new companions did not snore as badly, and he was able to get a good night's sleep.

The next day's expedition again offered rather muddy roads, but fortunately the rain had let up. Jed rode through 46 miles of Colorado that day, returning to Nebraska alongside the South Platte River at Julesburg Colorado. Passing through Sydney, a very rough town, Jed heard loungers on corners make comments as he rode through. After noticing they all wore six shooters, Jed fingered his pocket pistol as he rode through without stopping. Chappell was the dinner stop for the day, then Kimball, Nebraska, that evening—a distance of 140 miles for the day—despite the mud. This was a new record for our hero. When the hotel owner Told Jed that Sydney was an *outlaw town*, he realized that he was entering what he knew as the *Wild West*.

Leaving Kimball Jed and his Harley crossed the state line into Wyoming by midmorning, and began the upward climb. As he passed by Pine Bluffs, still climbing, the little Harley chugged towards Cheyenne, an increase in elevation of 3500 feet in under a hundred miles. Jed decided to stop in Cheyenne, a good-sized town, to see the sights and spend an extra day. By then Jed was looking pretty grubby, and had a difficult time finding a hotel that was not "all full." He visited the railroad station, checked the bike in, and cleaned himself up. Suddenly, there were vacancies to be had at the same hotels. He spent a great evening at a saloon, where he met some genuine cowboys, one of whom claimed to have known Billy the Kid and various other legendary characters. Whether this was the truth or not, Jed found the tales mesmerizing while he paid to keep his new companion's glass filled. It was just as well a days rest was the plan, as it would have been tough to ride the following morning. An afternoon stroll through town was about all that Jed could manage.

The road got much worse after Cheyenne. It leads upwards towards the summit at 8590 feet. The "road" was really a trail of loose stones, leading ever upwards, past the tree line, to the highest point of Jed's trip. At the summit, Jed spotted a surveyor's post. On it he discovered some engraved letters, crudely carved with a pocket knife: "G. A. Wyman, June 4, 1903, 11:30 a.m.—First motorcyclist to cross the Rockies, traveling from San Francisco to New York." Jed checked his pocket diary, and realized that Wyman had passed here four years ago, almost to the minute. To someone with a birthday every four years, it somehow seemed like an omen. Good or bad, he had no idea. The view was well worth the trip in his opinion, but it had been far from easy. He was plagued with belt slip, and, at the high altitude, the little engine had worked very hard. The power was barely up to the challenge. After enjoying the view, Jed began his descent, making Laramie by nightfall. It was the toughest day so far, but the most scenic. Laramie, with a population of 10,000, was located in a very lush setting. So far, Jed was impressed with the Wild West. It was rather difficult to leave Laramie after just two days, as it was a town of friendly people with to see and observe: drovers passing through, cowboys and ranchers meeting up at the local watering holes with many tall stories changing hands—all good fodder for a young, traveling motorcyclist. Jed's tales of adventure kept the locals entranced as well. He spent an evening with a local rancher just west of town the second night. The rancher's attractive daughter almost made him reconsider leaving, but he decided he could return later if the west coast proved disappointing. She waved him a farewell until the ranch house was out of sight.

The following day's run, although over very rough roads, was entirely downhill. This made for an easy ride, concluding at Walcott, a small town consisting of two saloons, a store, a railroad station and a good hotel. All of this was by virtue of the fact that two stage lines intersected with the railroad at this point. The hotel was quite clean and, typical of fine western hotels, had an outbuilding especially for the drunks who spent too much time in the saloons. Jed was wise enough to limit his intake that evening to ensure that he could keep his lodgings within the main building. In it was an excellent dining room, where he was able to speak with travelers from the stages and railroads about his adventures. One stage driver asked him if he thought that motor travel would ever replace stagecoaches. Jed postulated that the day would come when specially built automobiles, able to carry 14 or 16 passengers, would travel the stage roads much improved for this purpose. Other diners at the table looked askance at the driver and Jed. "We will live to see it," said Jed with some vision.

Riding westwards again, Jed passed through White Horse Canyon, named after an English *remittance man*, who, after having consumed a goodly amount of alcohol, rode his white horse over the precipice, crashing on the rocks 200 feet below. Remittance men were no-account sons of British aristocracy who were sometimes "sent abroad" to remove their embarrassing presence from their snooty relatives. Also, as was the English custom, estates were normally passed on to the eldest; the younger sons were encouraged to travel afar, and were often provided with *remittances* as compensation. Fortunately, not all ended up plastered on the rocks at the bottom of canyons. Many of them helped to "win the west".

Fort Fred Steele, an abandoned settlement of decrepit houses was the next stop, then Rawlins, where the road began to climb again. In between these two towns Jed came across an abandoned prairie schooner. He stopped to inspect the old wagon, imagining those people who had made this same trip long before him through unknown territory with Indians roaming the area, occasionally attacking the unwary. He was happy to be here in relatively civilized times. After Creston, where he stopped briefly for a meal, and in the direction of Rawlins, Jed came across a signpost marking the continental divide. He was rather surprised to find it situated on fairly flat ground, as opposed to a mountain ridge as he might have expected. Nevertheless, he was, he realized, looking somewhat downhill in both easterly and westerly directions. According to the signpost, San Francisco was 1100 miles westward. Jed still had a long way to go. Passing through Rawlins, he spent the night in Bitter Creek, Wyoming, where he had a decent meal in the boxcar restaurant. Although on the map, Bitter Creek exists strictly for the railroad hands; the hotel and restaurant were modified old boxcars, but the food and the bed were quite acceptable.

Heading out in the morning towards Rock Springs, Jed found the road mostly alkali sand, and rather badly cut up. While this slowed his progress, he reached Rock Springs by noon. After stopping for dinner, Jed took time to replenish his batteries and had his leather belt re-sewn at a local livery stable. Rock Springs had gained some notoriety over labor troubles, including the murder of Chinese workers at the local Union Pacific's coalmines. The afternoon's ride took Jed through the scenic settlement of Green River, pop. 1500, then through Marston, where he found the road terribly rocky. At Granger, a town of 200, he spent the night in the railroad hotel. Having pedaled a good five miles into Rock Springs with a broken belt, Jed was ready for a quiet night.

In the morning, after the usual hearty breakfast, Jed climbed, with some pedaling, to Altamont, elevation 7395 ft. This entailed passing through a railroad tunnel. The tunnel was full of smoke, indicating that a train had recently passed through. Jed, trusting his luck, figured that another train was unlikely to go through for a while. Fortunately, he was right. The roadway down towards Evanston, at 6759 ft., was made up mostly of baseball-sized rocks, making the ride very difficult. A couple of minor spills added to the drama. Jed was fascinated at the buttes, some of which had seashells protruding from them. He wrongly imagined how far the sea must have reached in pre-historic times, not realizing that the buttes had moved upwards. The stop that night was Evanston, with a population of 2000, his last night in Wyoming, before crossing into Utah. He visited a saloon that evening, as Jed knew that the Mormon settlements he would soon be passing through might not be willing to slake his thirst.

Motoring off towards Ogden, Utah, Jed passed the Castle Rocks, on the way to Echo City, where there was a Union Pacific Railroad Station, and very little else. The towering sandstone bluffs were the main attraction. Past Castle Rocks, he saw the Pulpit Rock, where Brigham Young had made a sermon during the Mormon pilgrimage. This meant little to Jed, as he was not a scholar in such concerns, preferring to focus on motorcycle matters, and to a lesser extent, young women. The road was rough, but was heading downhill toward Ogden with an elevation of 4301 ft., 2400 ft. lower than Evanston, Wyoming. By noon he had reached Echo City, a railroad settlement of 200, where he had dinner at the boxcar restaurant. Jed noticed that the Mormon Farmers with their wagons had little regard for him and would not yield him any way whatsoever. He wisely decided not to risk any arguments with them, as they were a tough lot, having been persecuted so much in their past.

Stopping in Ogden for the night, Jed retired to a hotel and spent some time working on the Harley, making minor adjustments, and cleaning off some mud. It certainly lacked the shine it had when he picked it up from Arthur Davidson at the "Shed," but it was running flawlessly. The City of Ogden had a population of 15,000, and had but one motorcyclist in 1903, when Wyman made his trip. Jed looked up S.C. Higgins, who had an Orient, accepting an invitation to stay the night. According to Higgins there were now about ten motorcycles in town, and some talk of starting a motorcycle club.

"I really like that Harley, Jed," said Higgins. "It looks in much better condition than Wyman's Yale California did when he reached here, and he'd only covered

833 miles. He was a pretty tough guy, riding that thing over those railroad ties with rigid front forks."

Jed told Higgins about his meeting up with Bill Harley and Arthur Davidson in Racine in 1896, and the Pennington Motorcycle. "Pennington has long since disappeared. Apparently he went to England, fleeced some more investors there, and died penniless in 1903. The Harley Davidson boys will do better though, I'm sure. They are taking a very conservative approach, and don't owe their souls to some bank."

Higgins agreed on the philosophy, but noted, "Indian is certainly the market leader here, though. Most of the boys in town are on Indians, and they even have a dealer. If you wanted one of your Harleys, you'd have to mail order it." The two enthusiasts argued the pros and cons of various machines into the wee hours, as they consumed a bottle of bourbon. Higgins was a self-confessed "Jack Mormon."

It was a bleary eyed start for Jed in the morning, but the sunny weather and fresh air soon revived him as he headed out of town, cruising along the flat, smooth dirt road following the north shore of the Great Salt Lake. About 50 miles out, he stopped by the shore, stripped, and went for a swim. He was amazed at how easy it was to float in the very salty water. When a family passed by in a wagon, Jed saw two young girls pointing at him and giggling, but the stern gentleman driving told them to keep their eyes front. Jed waited until the wagon passed into the distance before he got out of the water, dressed and headed out. He passed the wagon down the road and waved at the two girls. When there was no reaction, he blasted on down the road. Jed though he had better put some distance between himself and the Mormon farmer, who obviously was not pleased. The Harley carried its rider without mishap, along the smooth road to Terrace, where he took a room at the Southern Pacific Hotel. Here he enjoyed a good meal and an early evening. He slept like a log.

Traveling out of Terrace in the morning, Jed passed a great collection of dugouts and log houses made of railroad ties. They made acceptable living quarters for foreign laborers while they worked on the railroads. Some Indians used them as well, although most chose to live in teepees on the outskirts of the various towns. They seemed a sorry, unkempt lot. Having heard stories of fierce savages in his youth, Jed kept his revolver close at hand in case of attack. His fears were unfounded, as the "fierce savages" didn't appear to be motivated for any activity, fierce or otherwise. It was, he realized much later, a great tragedy for these once-proud people. With very little incident, Jed reached Wells, Nevada, that evening, to find a marvelous big hotel located in this town of 200. The dining room, which could have sat the entire population, had a simple menu: "Meal, 25 cts. Square Meal, 50 cts., or Gorge, 75 cts. Jed went for the 75-cent meal and could barely walk upstairs afterwards.

From Wells, Jed headed westward across the desert the following morning. All went well until Jed hit a washout, which was six feet deep and about ten feet across. The bike plunged into the hole, as Jed went flying, doing a somersault, before landing on his back on the other side of the washout. He laid there for a minute or two, the wind knocked out of him. He gathered himself up and, apart for some sore muscles, torn jacket, and a badly skinned hand, seemed to be in good order. Remarkably enough, the bike was relatively undamaged, although the front forks were bent backwards. He removed the front wheel and, with the help of a tree branch found nearby, was able to pry them back to a relatively straight position. Unfortunately, after the repair procedure, the front end springing no longer worked. "Damn!" he cursed to himself. "It will be a rough old trip until I can repair the forks properly." He had also damaged the throttle linkage again and had to settle for a jury-rigged repair. Jed decided he could live with the slightly bent handlebars, until he reached a suitable repair center with professional help.

The Harley readily started right up. Heading onward with more care, Jed noticed that the bike pulled to one side. He realized he would indeed need assistance. Upon reaching Elko, Jed found a livery stable with a rather talented blacksmith, who managed the repairs within two hours. This included straightening the forks and handlebars, and sorting out the suspension. The charge was ten dollars, which he was happy to pay, although he considered it to be a high price, just like the gasoline, which cost him 1.25 cents a gallon, by far the highest he had paid so far. He had averaged less than 40 cents per gallon up until then. Elko was an expensive place, so he decided to press on. The shiny gray paint that had graced the forks was now about half burnt off; the Harley was now showing the abuse of its trip. Jed encountered greasy, muddy roads in the afternoon, no doubt created by recent downpours. This made them almost impassable. Jed had to make frequent stops to scrape the mud from the wheels and belt pulleys to keep the machine running. He finally reached Carlin after dark, aided by a bright, full moon. Exhausted, he had a dreamless sleep on a bench at the railroad station.

Carlin to Humboldt was a rough desert trip, much as the day before. Humboldt proved to be a very pretty town, consisting of one structure: a house belonging to the station agent, who also acted as telegraph operator and keeper of the restaurant for passengers. Jed paid 50 cents for an excellent meal, double that charged elsewhere, but well worth the expense. He took a room in the loft of the building. Humboldt was a tiny oasis in the middle of the desert, created by the stationmaster. Jed was tempted to stay an extra day, but was anxious to make Reno, Nevada, his next planned overnight stop.

The following day was more desert travel. Temperatures were moderate and the riding conditions decent enough to make good time along mostly high ground. It was a desolate place, consisting of sand and tumbleweed for the most part. The only sign of life between the tiny settlements was the odd coyote or lizard. Jed charged on, hoping to get to more civilized country. The little Harley seemed anxious also, because it was running as well as it had since leaving Milwaukee.

Lovelock, at 3977 ft., was somewhat of an oasis, leading into the Forty Mile Desert of Nevada. This included Upsal, 4297 ft., Wadsworth, 4085 ft., and then Reno at 4497 ft. Jed, pressed onward, merely stopping for gasoline at Lovelock, as he had sandwiches provided by the station agent's wife at Humboldt. He did not realize that he was following the original wagon trails of the westward-bound pioneers. Later, the railroad engineers would often closely follow these same trails, and occasionally the rails had been laid directly on the trail routes. Jed was able to ride alongside the rails for many miles of this part of the desert.

He arrived in Reno about 7:30 pm, ready for a hearty meal and some needed relaxation. He had looked forward to getting off the bike, as it was quite cold. Snowflakes were beginning to fall, the first he'd seen since leaving home. He decided to wait out the weather if necessary, as Reno looked like a welcome place to spend an extra day if required. Reno was a town that had seen better days during the gold rush of 1849, but it still had a few decent hotels. Jed took a room, had a good meal with a couple of beers before settling in for a much need rest.

The early morning skies were remarkably clear and sunny and there was no evidence of snow. Jed decided to head out early; he was close to California—approaching the last part of his trip. He left soon after daybreak to begin the upward climb through the Sierra Mountains. Unlike Wyman's ride, four years previously, Jed encountered very little snow near the summit. Like Wyman, Jed used the snow sheds to avoid what snow there was. He passed over the summit that evening, ending up at Immigrant Gap. From now on, the remainder of the ride would all be downhill. Following the railroad the following day, Jed arrived at Sacramento, the capital of California. He looked over the southward route and located the Los Angeles basin, where he hoped to make a new home for himself—perhaps a new life.

Without Wyman's route to follow, Jed decided that the easiest way to get to the Los Angeles area was to follow the Union Pacific line southward from Sacramento, by-passing San Francisco altogether, as he was anxious to reach his destination. With that in mind, he started out early in the morning, following the tracks. Jed found a wide, smooth roadbed, wide enough that he had to take to the rails only occasionally, usually on trestles crossing creeks and gorges. The weather was fabulous for those last three days of his ride; he passed well-run ranches, farms, and even an occasional winery, with many Chinese and Mexican laborers toiling in the fields.

Finally, Jed reached the Los Angeles basin, where he rode the dusty, worn Harley, its tires worn through to the cords, into the town of Los Angeles. He calculated that he had averaged 85 miles per gallon on his expedition. During the trip, the bike had suffered the bent forks and handlebars, two broken valves, three spark plugs, two tires, four tubes, and a half a dozen sets of batteries.

He found a hotel to his liking and began to think about how to make a new beginning in this welcoming, broad region where the only west remaining was the Pacific Ocean.

CHAPTER NINE

THE FIRST TASTE OF RACING
AND THE MATTER OF LUCY

Jed Fleming found the Los Angeles basin very much to his liking. He found a good rooming house with a landlady who was not only an excellent cook, but also she and her husband had cheery personalities and treated him almost like a son. The weather was warm and mostly sunny, and the air was fresh and clean, a perfect climate for a motorcyclist. The basin area consisted of several small towns close to one another with an agricultural economic base. Hundreds of acres of orange groves, grapefruit trees, dates and various other crops surrounded the area. Fresh produce was abundant and always available, something Jed had never experienced. He was particularly fond of the oranges and grapefruits: he ate so many oranges when he first arrived that his complexion took on an orange-like hue.

Jed treated his trusty Harley to a full refurbishment. After completely dismantled it in the yard behind the rooming house, he took the frame and forks to a local cycle shop for re-enameling. He decided to stick with the "Renault Grey" color again, as it didn't show the dirt as much as some other colors. He wrote to Bill Harley to order a set of handlebars to replace the bent ones, as well as parts needed to fix the throttle control and new bearings and rings. Bill sent a postcard, showing a picture of the Harley Davidson factory with yet another addition. There was a note explaining that he was sending a new type of throttle control, which he called a twist—grip: "Try it out Jed, and let me know what you think. I think it's an improvement, but Arthur isn't convinced. We'd like a few fellows to try them out before we decide on fitting them to all the bikes." Upon fitting and using it, Jed decided that the twist grip was an improvement over the previous loose wire control; he replied to Bill commenting with enthusiasm for the new part. The new cable control, with piano wire inside a flexible cable, would serve Harley Davidson for many decades.

It didn't take Jed long to find and become acquainted with other motorcyclists in the area. The Agricultural Park in Los Angeles was a hotbed of activity, with motorcycle racing on a one—mile horse track the main attraction. He was soon on a first-name basis with local heroes: *Miles a Minute* Collins, who had been the first to lap the track at 60 mph; Paul, *Dare Devil*, Derkum; *Shrimp*, Burns and a host of others. Their race bikes, with no brakes or clutches, were kept for that purpose only. Jed decided he would need a racing machine in addition to his Harley, which was his transportation. He was in no hurry, as he wished to make the right decision when the time came. He hung around the track where he helped fetch fuel, pump up tires and did a bit of fettling for the boys to hone his tuning skills.

"Paul Derkum on Indian, 1908"

One February Saturday, in the winter of 1908, Derkum said, "Hey Fleming, lets see if you can ride a real motorcycle. You can take out my Indian for a few practice laps." Derkum had one of the new Indian twins, fitted with the latest mechanically operated intake valves—a most serious machine. Known as the *Monkey on a Stick* model, the seat was positioned over the rear wheel, extended rearward on a long rod. Derkum himself had helped Indian develop it for racing.

"OK, don't forget you don't have any brakes or throttle control," Derkum explained, "Once the thing lights up you are on your way. You have a kill button on the handlebars to cut the ignition, but you drift sideways on the corners and that will help slow you down. Get on, and we'll give you a shove."

The rest of the fellows gathered to watch. "This should be good." smiled Burns. The Indian started after a fast push by Derkum and Burns, and the little twin leapt forward in a cloud of blue smoke. Jed was quite surprised at the acceleration it had compared to his Harley single. Almost immediately, when he approached the first turn, Jed hit the kill switch, and then quickly released it half way around. The sudden power kicked out the rear end of the machine, immediately sending the machine into a slide. When Jed hit the switch again, the bike straightened out, and he almost high sided it. As he came around past the gathered racers, he saw they were really enjoying the spectacle.

"I can master this!" Jed said to himself. He did a few more laps, and soon got used to the kill switch to control his speeds and the sliding to some degree. He was just beginning to gain some confidence when something unexpected happened: he was beginning to feel uncomfortably warm in the area of his crotch. He did another lap before the pain increased to the intolerable level. Discovering his trousers on fire, Jed lost control, letting the bike slide sideways into the hay bales. His trousers were on fire. Shrimp Burns ran over with a pail of water, throwing it over Jed. With another pail, Derkum doused the Indian as Jed blacked out.

The next 24 hours were all but a painful haze. Jed would later recall being carried off the track, laid in the back of a spectator's wagon driven to hospital. His burns were attended to, and so was his upper body; he had broken an arm as well his collarbone. He hadn't noticed these injuries at first due to the pain of the burn. Later, when woke from a drugged sleep, he opened his eyes to see Derkum at this bedside. "What the hell happened?" Jed managed to ask.

"The gas tank split at the back, probably because of your lousy riding," said Derkum with a sly smile. "Some fuel poured down onto the engine and was ignited by the exhaust flames coming from those ported cylinders. The rest of it ended up soaking your pants and your balls. The whole thing was pretty spectacular." With that, Derkum reached into a paper bag he was holding and extracted a bottle of bourbon. He poured two glasses, also found in the bag, and handed one to Jed. "Here's to your new nickname. From now on you will be known as *Fireball Fleming.* You are more than welcome to join our little group. We have a little deal with the track owners, and have a piece of the gate. You'll have to earn some money anyway to pay for my Indian you wrecked. You'll have to get a race bike of your own if you want a decent share of the take."

Jed, newly named as Fireball, and Daredevil had pretty well polished off the bottle when a rather stern faced nurse entered the room. "There will be no drinking here!" she said, as she ushered Derkum out of the room. "We need to change these dressings."

Much to Fireball's embarrassment, the nurse lifted the sheets and removed the dressings. She then took a jar of ointment and began to apply it to his wounds. In spite of the pain and the embarrassment, he began to feel somewhat aroused, as that particular part of his anatomy was remarkably undamaged. "We'll have none of that, young man," said the nurse as she delivered a sharp blow to his groin. The offending member collapsed immediately. Fireball's face was on fire. For the next four days, the exercise was repeated, but the blow to the groin was only necessary once more, as Jed strove to control himself. On the fifth day, the 29th of February, a different nurse entered the room: this one was younger, prettier and had a winning smile. Blond curls tumbled out from her nurse's cap. "This is really going to be tough," thought Jed. He wanted no more blows to his groin.

"Hi there! My name's Miss Meredith. Lets see what we have here, shall we?" With that, she rolled back the sheets, and began to remove the dressings. "I think you are coming along nicely," she said. Miss Meredith then took the ointment and began gently applying it to his nether regions. "O my God, here we go again," thought Jed, preparing himself for a blow that did not happen.

"That's not exactly where I'm burnt, said Jed, desperately trying to gain control without success. Miss Meredith continued her ministrations then stood back and surveyed her work. "There we are. I think that will do nicely." Miss Meredith then turned to Jed, and with a smile began to unbutton her uniform, and was soon standing there without a stitch of clothing on. She was the prettiest thing Jed had ever seen.

Miss Meredith then promptly leapt onto the bed, straddling Jed in the process. As she moved above him, she purred, "Happy Birthday, Fireball, From Daredevil Derkum and the boys at the track." His injuries were temporarily forgotten.

The next morning, pain returned to his lower body as a result of the previous day's strenuous activities—and to his head as a result of the bottle that Miss Meredith had brought to celebrate his birthday in the afterglow of their activities. The real nurse returned, and was none too pleased at his condition, so he wasn't released from hospital for several more days. The breaks in his arm and shoulder began to really bother him as the burns healed; he was a sorry sight when he hobbled out of the hospital, but made his way to the track nonetheless in a hired carriage. He had to give thanks for one of the best birthdays so far, his 6th. It was almost as good as getting the Orient on his 4th.

As it was Saturday morning, the boys were out practicing, but when they saw Jed arrive, they all cut their ignitions, and coasted around to where he was standing at the rail. "How was the birthday, Fireball?" asked Derkum with a broad smile. Somewhat embarrassed, Jed replied, "Miss Meredith was a wonderful young lady." The boys dissolved in peals of laughter. "Miss Meredith my ass!" howled Collins. "That's Loose Lucy, one of the whores that hangs around the track. She'll drop her knickers for anyone with six bits, even ole' Shrimp, here!" With that Shrimp got off his bike, and pounded Collins on the arm, supported with smiles all around. Jed knew he would have fun with this gang, even though he wouldn't be able to ride for a while. He also decided not to go anywhere without at least six bits in his pocket in case he met Lucy again.

Chapter Ten

THE BIRTH OF BOARD TRACK RACING

Fireball spent most of the spring in slow, painful recovery, as the breaks were painful after the burns healed up. During the convalescence he was surprised to receive a letter from his mother.

Dear Jedidiah:

I got your address from that no-good uncle of yours, with some difficulty. It is very hard to get hold of him, as he spends most of his time when he's not making money, taking strong drink, and cavorting with loose women. My poor sister has left him, and is now living a proper God fearing life with Harold and I on the farm. She is much better off without that evil man.

Speaking of your uncle, you have become a good understudy. That poor girl, whose father is a friend of Harold's, was left in a family way by you, much to our embarrassment. She was a stubborn girl, and insisted in keeping the child, a boy. Thankfully, the family rallied around, and found the unfortunate girl a respectable husband, who was willing to take the child as his own. Your bastard offspring now has an opportunity to lead a respectable life, no thanks to you.

I hope you are able to repent your ways, and lead a good God fearing life in California, far from us here.

Your Loving Mother

After a second reading, Jed crumpled the letter and tossed it in the woodstove. He then poured himself a glass of *strong drink*, smiled with fondness for Uncle George and contemplated meeting Lucy Meredith again.

As summer approached, Jed was able to get back on his Harley and ride to the track, although racing was still out of the question. If Fireball Fleming was going to make a name for himself, it would come later. He passed the time helping with the bikes in the pits, where he learned that the various manufacturers and suppliers were taking more than a passing interest in their activities. Tires, parts, and even complete machines, appeared with little or no money changing hands, This was particularly so for Derkum, who, in addition to being virtually unbeatable on the track, had a bit of the showman in him and was quite the salesman. Derkum was very much into self promotion. At the end of the year, he put his Indian on display at Donahoo Edmonds Sporting Goods Store with the trophies he had won. Jed put pressure on Derkum for a bike, and became owner of Daredevil's extra 08 Indian Twin, the one that had caught fire. It was nicknamed *The Fireball Special* by the boys. Derkum had a new deal for 1909: he was now riding for the Thor factory.

In September of 1908, a big Lozier touring car pulled up to the track after the day's racing, and Derkum called the boys over to trackside to meet his new friend and business associate.

"Fellows, I want you to meet Jack Prince. He has some ideas which I think you will all be excited about." Introductions were made all around while Prince drew a blanket off the rear seat of the Lozier, uncovering a supply of beer, whiskey and Moxie soft drinks. "Help yourselves, boys," he offered with a sweeping hand gesture.

As they relaxed and became acquainted, Prince asked the boys, "How many of you fast lads began as bicycle racers?" The entire group raised their hands. "You all know, then, the value of a velodrome track. A few years back, we were running motorcycles on those velodromes, but these modern machines became too fast, so we took to the horse tracks. You are now going so fast, that you have to keep cutting your engines to make the corners, or you will slide out, right, Shrimp?" he asked Burns. When Shrimp nodded his assent, Prince asked, "What was the advantage of the velodromes?" Jed raised his hand, remembering his adventures with the Pony Star. "Banked corners and a hard surface" he replied. "Exactly!" said Prince.

"What we are going to do, boys, is build a wooden *motordrome*, right here at the Coliseum. It will be like a velodrome, but it will be much larger, with steeper banking, and it will only take 3½ laps to complete a mile. It will also be wide enough that five or six bikes can run abreast. The surface will be of 2x4 planks placed on edge, supported underneath with trestle-like construction. With the banked surface, these modern machines of yours will be able to reach their full potential. I see new speed records being broken, and huge crowds gathered to watch you modern gladiators on your iron steeds, traveling at 100 miles an hour! Board track racing will be America's newest, and most exciting spectator event ever, and you will be the entertainers!"

"Wow", said Shrimp. "Count me in!" The others all responded with equal enthusiasm.

Jack Prince got a set of drawings out from the Lozier's tonneau cover and spread them out on the long hood of the car. "As you can see," he said, "this project will involve a lot of carpentry. I'm willing to hire any of you lads to build the track, and you can also race there on weekends. We will work twelve-hour days, as we want it to be up and running next season. I will superintend the project, and Derkum here will be foreman. Who's on?" Three quarters of them volunteered, including Jed. "It's my right arm that's a bit useless, but I can sure drive nails with my left," he exclaimed. "Fair enough, boys," replied Prince, "You can all start work the day the trainload of lumber and spikes arrive!" With that, he polished off the dregs of the remaining whiskey straight from the bottle, while Derkum cranked the Lozier for him. He sped away in a cloud of dust.

Fireball had to have his arm reset. This, along with the other broken bones, healed slowly. It was a pretty tough summer and fall for him: watching the lads out on the track—watching, but not doing. It was later that fall before he was able to ride the Harley again. He was thankful for the twist grip setup that Bill Harley had sent him, as he managed to control the bike with his arm in a cast. The open ported racing Indian would have to wait for a while.

"Jack Prince & Paul Derkum, 1908"

In September, things started to get interesting, especially when forty carloads of lumber and spikes arrived at the track. The spikes alone filled over half a railcar. The cars were shunted onto the nearby spur line where the boys began to unload the wood and move it to the site of the new track in wagons. Jed's injured arm made it difficult to do heavy lifting, so he became Derkum's assistant. The building materials were placed around the periphery of the track site in an oval shape, so as to minimize the further carrying of the long lengths of boards.

The first activity was to pour the footings. The square holes were dug by hand, and lined with timber on the sides. They mixed the concrete with rake and shovel in wheelbarrows before pouring it into the forms. While the concrete was still wet, they inserted bolts into the sloppy material, leaving the threaded ends protruding upwards. After setting up overnight, the boys removed the forms, backfilled the spaces around the footings gravel and compacted this by hand with heavy tools. The compactors consisted of a heavy iron plate with a flattened bottom and a t-shaped handle protruding upwards. It took two men to lift the device and drop it on the gravel, until all was compacted to Derkum's satisfaction. The work was backbreaking.

"You lucky bastard!" said Shrimp to Fireball, as his little body toiled under the weight. Fortunately for Shrimp and the others, the footings were completed in under a week. As Derkum explained, the footings were needed to not only support the weight of the structure, but to prevent it from sliding outward from the centrifugal force created by the force of the machines, which would be traveling at speeds never seen before. The boys were all young and pretty tough and not afraid of work. Also, they were all very anxious to try out the completed motordrome.

Building the wooden portion was far more interesting than preparing footings, as the boys were able to see far more progress from their efforts. The trestle portions and underpinning were made from rough-cut 4x4 lumber. They bored holes by hand in the base of the beams with brace and bit, then placed the beams over the bolts in the footings and secured them with nuts and washers. The beams would support the upper track structure.

Jack Prince began arriving on the site during this phase. He set up his transit and level to establish position and elevation of the racing surface. It was a complicated procedure, as the transition from the straightaway through the banking had to be smooth. They placed uprights with marked grades, which Prince called *grade stakes*.

The surface then began to take shape: 2x4 lumber laid on edge formed the surface, running in the line in the direction that racing motorcycles would soon follow. Being ambidextrous, Jed was able to play a part in this part, pounding nails with his left arm, silencing the protests of his pal, Shrimp, about not doing his share of sweating.

Once they had finished the surface, the boys were very anxious to get on the track and try it out. "No way," smiled Prince, "there's no point in wearing the thing out before we have the stands in place. Not only that, but I'd hate like hell to see any of you gladiators getting killed without any paying customers sitting there to watch it all—and telling their friends, so we will get more customers." Little did he know the truth of his light-hearted comment. Not unlike the Roman Coliseum, the board tracks would soon see their share of blood.

The stands faced the straighter sections of the track, although even the "straights" were slightly banked, as the track was actually somewhat egg shaped with no straight sections like a horse track. Unlike an egg, however, both end sections were identical. Outside the high end banked surface was a walkway for additional viewing. There was also a light rail fence running alongside the outer surface, presumably keep the machines from flying off the track. There was an access passageway beneath the track, allowing machines and riders to enter the infield, which would be used as the pits.

Derkum's new Thor racer arrived just prior to the completion of the track in the spring of 1909. Jed looked at it with some envy, as it was longer and lower than his Indian. It had a big twin 61 cu. in. displacement, as opposed to Jed's Indian of 37 inches. "A day late and a dollar short," he mused, "I haven't even ridden my bike, and it's already obsolete. Damn!"

As the stands neared completion, Jack Prince showed up with a professional photographer. The photographer staged several shots, with bikes and riders on the track with the appearance of actual racing. Thin lines attached to the machines allowed for a realistic lean, giving the appearance of great speed. Derkum, of course, was positioned in the lead. The pictures appeared in all the local papers, promising thrills, spills, and more, on the new *Motordrome*.

Jack Prince, a seasoned promoter, soon lined up various exclusives for suppliers of services to the spectators—even before the first engine was started. Boys selling peanuts, for example, were required to pay a percentage to the track and even had to pay their own way in. The racers and organizers got their peanuts for free, of course. The supply of soft drinks came from the Moxie Beverage Company in exchange for the exclusive rights; a fee accrued to Prince. The Moxie salesman delivered his wares in one of the Moxie "Horsemobiles". The Horsemobile driven by the salesman, was a Lozier touring automobile with the seats removed. In the car was a full-sized horse constructed of wire mesh and plaster, this particular one was painted to look like an Appaloosa. The horse was saddled up western style, and the salesman was dressed accordingly. A steering wheel protruded from the horse's mane, while other controls were located within the stirrups and on the side of the horse. The feeling was that you had to have "a lot of Moxie" to be a Moxie salesman and to drive a Horsemobile. And so an expression became part of everyday speech. Other supplies were delivered in more conventional ways. Delivery of alcohol was very discrete. Various manufacturers offered sponsorships to the riders, not just companies making motorcycles, but tire manufacturers, companies such as "Oilzum" and so forth. Drummers for these firms were at the races regularly.

"Moxie Horsmobiles go to work"

Before the track opened for business, Jack Prince had the photographer shoot a group of riders, including Fleming, posed on the track in a position hunched over the bikes as though they were racing. Supporting thin cords, running from the bikes to the edge of the track, made them appear to be leaning over at fearsome angles. The pictures taken were used to promote the grand opening. One showed Derkum in the lead aboard his new Reading Standard, another make that sponsored him.

"Posing at the Track. Derkum in lead"

As the track neared completion, Lucy Meredith appeared one day to oversee progress and to talk to the boys. Jed saw her again professionally; soon these expenses were part of his monthly budget. Strangely, they became quite good friends, and although it was a bit like a romance to Jed, there were no bargains. Whenever he wanted a "poke," as the expression of the day went, he paid full tariff like everyone else. Lucy, a jolly sort with a sense of humor, was good company in addition to her other skills. She had a few friends with similar motivations who Jed sampled, but Lucy remained his favorite. Lucy said she was only selling pokes to get ahead. She had aspirations of becoming an actress and wished to star in those new fangled 5-cent moving pictures that were appearing in theaters in the town. "Just think, Jed, you only have to perform once, and you can appear over and over again. I think moving pictures have a big future." How right she was.

Prior to the opening of the track, two easterners arrived, one of whom would come to unseat Derkum as the fastest man on two wheels. They were Jake DeRosier and Freddy Huyck, each with new Indians provided by the factory in Springfield. Jake DeRosier, a French Canadian, showed a wicked sense of humor. Fireball warmed to him instantly. De Rosier was popular with the ladies and, when he raced, wore ballet tights and light footwear. As he said, "It makes you go faster, by gar! The Indian, she is a fast one!" The Indian machines had the new loop frame and 61 cu.in engines. While they were longer and lower than Jed's monkey on a stick bike, he was determined to do his best with his little steed.

To generate some excitement, a series of match races between Derkum and DeRosier were set up at the Agricultural dirt track during the winter of '08 and '09 with both riding Indians. With DeRosier winning three out of three races, Derkum claimed DeRosier's factory-prepared machine gave him an unfair advantage. Derkum, nevertheless, had finally met his match.

The new board track opened to a sellout crowd as predicted by Jack Prince, but the star hometown favorite, Derkum, was only in the lead on the promotional posters created by Prince. Jake DeRosier set four world records on opening weekend. The following weekend, Jake established two more records: he covered 10 miles in 8.348 minutes, breaking the previous record by 26.2 seconds, a straight-line race at Daytona Beach ridden by A.G. Chapple on an Indian the previous winter. The second record was 20 miles in 17.014 minutes, another record, giving De Rosier the win as well.

Fireball ran in all of these events, running well back, but was pleased to finish in the company of these great riders. He was surprised to discover that his Indian, which was an experimental one with mechanical inlet valves, could almost pull as well as Derkum's Thor, with its larger engine, but with atmospheric inlets. He lacked Derkum's skill and nerve, though, so Daredevil got well ahead of him. Jed found the speeds very intimidating, especially given the closeness of the other riders on the track. Close friends became fierce no-holds-barred competitors: even his pal Shrimp, as he passed by, kicked Jed's front wheel causing a tank "slapper." He almost crashed, but somehow recovered. "What the hell did you do that for,

Shrimp?" Jed hollered, "I ought to take a round out of you!" Shrimp was as angry as he was. "I was lapping you, you idiot! I had that frog DeRosier and his fancy pants in my sights and was gaining on him when you got in my way! Do that again, and you'll be into the boards!"

While Jed had no desire to crash and break more bones, he found the racing to be great fun. With open exhausts, total loss oiling and, in some cases, ported cylinders with exhaust exiting through holes drilled in the cylinder bases, the smoke and oil fumes made visibility difficult as the races wore on. There was no breeze on those first couple of weekends, and the smoke sat in the bowl of the track, much as smog would settle in the Los Angeles Basin in future decades.

The curves of the motordrome allowed the motorcycles to go much faster than they had on level horse tracks. After a few weekends of racing, the boards became slippery with oil fumes from the open-ported engines, making the riding increasingly difficult. The only relief from the oil occurred when an occasional rainstorm cleared the track after a fashion.

Most of the racers were reasonably good mechanics. They kept their own machines in order, mostly with help from the various manufacturers and suppliers who had agents on hand to help riders perform well with their products. Fireball, one of the slower riders with an obsolete machine, had to fend for himself. He was able to hone his mechanical and tuning skills to a fairly high degree. This earned him the respect of DeRosier, a hopeless mechanic. Thus their friendship grew: Jed kept the great man's bike in good fettle, while Jake gave Jed tips on getting around the track in a hurry. Fireball Fleming's tuning shop, located under the track became a fixture. He bought an old hand-cranked drill press and was soon drilling cylinders for porting. These holes, at the base of the cylinders just above the piston crown and positioned at bottom dead center, allowed exhaust to exit, causing a vacuum, which aided the incoming charge from the carburetor when the intake valve opened. This tuning trick was discovered more by accident than anything else, as the original intent was just to create more noise, flames, smoke and showmanship. In later years, when the concept of valve overlap was understood, porting of cylinders was abandoned. Jed, recognizing the value of engine balancing, had an old apothecary's balance which he used on rods and pistons. Working on DeRosier's machine, he soon recognized the difference between an over-the-counter machine and the meticulously prepared ones supplied to the factory riders. Fireball gradually realized he lacked the killer instinct to be a constant winner like his friend DeRosier. Nevertheless he was happy to be a participant and realized his great calling might just be in engine preparation and tuning. He really enjoyed the mechanical work, particularly on those factory racers.

In experimenting with his own machine, for example, Jed had discovered that overlapping the valve openings at top dead center on the inlet stroke gave him slightly more power. He could do this with his mechanically opened intakes on the Indian and noticed that it pulled as well as Derkum's larger Thor, with its atmospheric intakes.

Also recognizing he was outclassed by the likes of DeRosier, Derkum, who had no desire to play second fiddle, became race manager and announcer. He spoke through a large megaphone to the crowd; the megaphone was embossed with the sign "Daredevil Derkum". He had a variety of megaphones with various other signs advertising Indian, Flying Merkel, Thor, and others, and would use a particular sign according to which company was the most financially generous at the time. Derkum introduced riders and alluded to the spills and thrills the crowd would soon witness to raise the level of anticipation and excitement.

"The young gladiators"

The new sport of board track racing took the public by storm. In the days when the average car was capable of 35 mph, to see motorcycles traveling at close to three times that speed was exciting indeed. It was an obviously dangerous sport as well, with riders wearing little in the way of protective clothing—and riding machines with no brakes. Most riders wore little more than street clothes and caps turned backwards with goggles to protect them from the oil fumes and the odd flying bit of metal when an engine exploded ahead of them. While the odd leather flying helmet showed up, there was no head protection to speak of until leather football helmets appeared. One of the most frequent injuries was from slivers picked up when a bike crashed. Sliding along on the rough timber, a rider could pick up many slivers in his body, some of which were a foot or more in length. Surprisingly, most riders didn't even wear gloves.

Jack Prince gathered the boys one Saturday night after the racing was over. With his arm around his right-hand man, Derkum, he announced that a second track was to go up, this one at Playa Del Ray, west of Los Angeles. "You boys are going so fast, that we need a bigger track, a mile in length. Any of you that want to earn some extra money are more than welcome to work on it. As you race, you will develop more fame, and make more money. The manufacturers and suppliers are swarming for your participation in using their products. That brings up a point, boys. You know who the big players are, and who support us financially. Occasionally someone shows up with one of these oddball makes that offer us no financial support. Run them into the boards, boys. That should be the job of some of the slower guys at the rear, like you, Fireball. Don't forget: we are in show business, and the crowds like to see those crashes. If you can't win races, try to do or cause something spectacular out there to earn your keep. Let's face it, you young guys have come off many times without serious injury, because you are a tough lot. Try not to light your balls on fire, like Fireball here. Don't interfere with the fast guys, though. We need those speed records. Each time we establish a new one, the attendance goes up."

With that, he stepped into the Locomobile, to drive off down the road, but not until Derkum cranked it up and lit the acetylene lamps for him.

CHAPTER ELEVEN

BOARD TRACK RACING—A NEW AMERICAN OBSESSION

In 1908 the Hendee Manufacturing Company introduced a 61-inch twin racer featuring a mechanical valve gear like Fireball's little twin. In the hands of riders like Jake DeRosier and Derkum, this innovation allowed for increasingly greater speeds, as Jack Prince had predicted. Morty Graves showed up at the Agricultural Park track with a potent 61 cu. in. Minerva, a Belgian make in the single-cylinder class. The *Flying Merkel* made its initial appearance in Ohio, piloted by a young apprentice in the test department named Maldwyn Jones. Fireball soon discovered that his little twin was capable of greater speeds, at least with him on board, than it had achieved on the dirt track. With rapt attention and fascination, he watched the development of these newer engines. At the same time, his attention was on keeping Jake's machinery in top condition focusing on refining his tuning skills. Occasionally Jake would allow Fireball to track test his machines—to experience first hand the amazing rate of development in engine advances.

In 1909, another European machine appeared at the Coliseum Motordrome. A pair of NSU 6 HP twins with belt drive, ridden by Arthur Mitchel and Morty Graves, proved to be very speedy indeed. Graves later claimed that he could ride it flat out on the boards—leaning it over so far that the four-inch wide engine pulley would run on the surface, giving him, in effect, a third stabilizing "wheel." Obviously, he was riding very much at the limit. Belt drive was the favored system in use in England and Europe in those days, while most American machines were adopting the chain drive systems pioneered by Indian.

During this period, however, Harley Davidson promoted the flat belt drive, common to agricultural machinery at the time and readily accessible. As it was, Bill Harley and Arthur Davidson still showed little interest in racing. Fireball was still using his '07 Harley Single for dependable transportation. He well knew that if Harley Davidson were to seriously enter the racing arena, they would be a major force.

Oscar Hedstrom appeared at the Coliseum Motordrome to see his star rider in action. He approached Jed Fleming with an interesting proposal: "I well remember how you caught on to all things mechanical when we first met, Jed. Jake thinks very highly of your tuning skills, and as we both know, he's a hopeless mechanic. I'd like you to travel with Jake, and help him keep his bikes in fine order. You are good friends, and I think that is paramount if you are to be together that much."

Hedstrom offered Jed an attractive retainer. Then, as they walked together out of the motordrome, he saw Jed's bike. "What on earth is that thing?" said Hedstrom with a smile, as he examined the Harley. "I think we had better get you an Indian for transportation. We want you to have dependability." Within a couple of weeks, Jed was in possession of a new 1910 Big Twin Indian Roadster at a very attractive price. The Harley went to a new owner shortly thereafter.

The new Indian featured a two-speed gear and clutch, a revelation to Jed. With the two speeds, the usual pedals were redundant. To start the bike, the rider had to either spin the rear wheel when it was on its rear stand, or run with it with the clutch engaged with the hand lever, then hopping on board, while releasing the lever, before the bike left town without you. Kick starters were a couple of years away from introduction. It sounds a bit difficult, but it was an easy procedure for a fit man like Fireball. As he blasted down the road on the new roadster, he sensed that the fast cross-country rides that he dreamed about were within sight. The roads, however, would require a good deal of improvement.

When he heard of Jed's new arrangement with Hedstrom, Shrimp Burns told him, "You know, Fireball, I'd worry about you spending so much time with a guy that wears ballet tights if I didn't know you spend half your dough cavorting with Loose Lucy and her pals. I guess you're as normal as the rest of us." Shrimp may have had a point. Although he and Lucy had become quite good friends, she still charged him pretty well full tariff, justified by her desire to get into "show business." She certainly had talent, but it wasn't for public consumption. She was often at the track and always gave Jed first refusal for her services. He liked the arrangement, as there were no long-term commitments. She was good company in the afterglow as well.

During the 1910 season, Jake De Rosier, with Fireball as his constant companion, won hundreds of events across the country. When there was an extra factory bike available, Fireball joined the ride, although he was no match for Jake. Jed could usually be found running at the back of the pack, enjoying himself nonetheless. His own "monkey on a stick" '08 racer had expired in impressive fashion at the new Play del Ray Motordrome. The track was so large that Jed ran it wide open longer than the engine could hold. He had it tuned finely to the very outer limit. The engine exploded so spectacularly that it took out at once the crankcases and cylinders, while a connecting rod cut the bottom loop of the frame. Jed slid down the track, picking up a body full of slivers and cracking a couple of ribs. As the medics lifted the stretcher into the wagon, Jack Prince appeared, and placing a bottle of bourbon beside Jed, said. "Nice piece of work, Fireball. The crowds loved that one. Are you OK?"

Fireball was back in action within a week, his torso wrapped massively in tape.

CHAPTER TWELVE

THE ISLE OF MAN TOURIST TROPHY RACE

In early 1911, when Oscar Hedstrom called Jake and Jed to his office at "the Wigwam" in Springfield, Massachusetts, the two wasted no time in boarding the east-bound train. A first-time visitor, Fireball was amazed at the size of the factory. It was an international business, as Indians were exported worldwide. He thought back to his visit to the little building where the Harleys were built. Oscar Hedstrom led them on a tour, mostly for Jed's benefit, as Jake had been there many times, then announced that the British Agent, Billy Wells, had suggested that Indian send Jake and some specially prepared machines to the Isle of Man for a race that was run on public roads. In addition, Hedstrom intended to send Jake's trusty 1911 board-track racer, # 21 to run on the Brooklands racetrack, located at Weybridge, west of London. A series of match races would be held between the Indian, and the Collier Brothers' *Matchless*, which was the British industry's most formidable offering. According to Wells, success in this Isle of Man Tourist Trophy Race, or TT, as it was commonly known, was the best advertising available for motorcycle sales, particularly in Europe. The TT originated in 1907. In 1911 a new, longer course was laid out, stretching 36 miles in length. The race consisted of seven continuous laps.

"I think we may have an advantage with our chain drive and two-speed gear," said Hedstrom. "Wells has a few local boys who have ridden in the TT before to back up Jake. The rules in the "senior" event, call for 500 cc singles, 580cc twins, or *multis*. Most of the Brit bikes are still running belts and single gearing. With a lot of automatic intakes still being run over there, they have given an advantage to the multis, as automatic intakes work better with larger cylinders. I plan to prepare twin cylinder racers, based on our little twin engine, which we will reduce to 580ccs by altering the bore size. We need special frames as we don't catalog a two—speed little twin, but Wells figures we can get away with it. Strictly speaking, they won't be production models, but, if put to the test, we could make a few for sale. For the match races at Brooklands, we need to make some modifications to # 21. Fireball, if you would be so kind: start by removing the pedal cranks and fit foot pegs, then shorten the front spring, as Brooklands is very rough concrete. According to Wells, things need to be stiffened up." Oscar said that he regretted he could not justify the expense of an ocean passage for Jed, as Wells had good mechanical backup. Fireball decided it was time to work on Uncle George again.

As Jed expected, George was keen on this adventure. Asking what ship Jake was to be on, George quickly booked first-class accommodation for them on same voyage as Jake on the *Lusitania*. While Jake was booked in second class, George said that he would get Jake upstairs for social events, as he was a major investor in Cunard Lines.

Departure was in late April of 1911. Jed and Jake followed George up the gangway on board the second largest ship in the world, second only to her almost identical sister ship, the *Mauritania*, which had been launched two months later than the Lusitania. The 30,000-ton Lusitania was the holder of both Blue Ribands, however, awarded for the fastest trans-Atlantic crossing in each direction. She was an awesome sight with her four enormous funnels and great length, moored in New York that day. Once aboard, they were separated: Jed and George were ushered to their first class staterooms, while Jake was directed to his somewhat more modest second-class accommodations. As Jed checked out his large room, complete with marble bathtub, gold plated faucets and fancy décor, he reflected that the previous luxury of the private rail car was comparatively basic. The Lusitania was like a floating palace. "She runs on steam, Jed, just like my new Stanley Gentlemen's Speedy Roadster," said George.

The ship left the dock amidst much fanfare. Departing passengers threw paper streamers, while there was much waving from friends on shore. After being eased down the East River by relatively miniscule steam tugs, the ship steamed away under the power of her own four screws. The voyage had begun: the open Atlantic Ocean vas visible over the bow of the massive ship.

George and Jed went to the deck immediately below to locate Jake. George had arranged a tour of the vessel with the Captain. Their escort was a smartly dressed second officer.

"We'll start at the bottom, gentlemen. The boilers produce the power for the ship. As well as the engines, there is the hotel load, the power required to heat water, keep the radiators in the staterooms nice and warm and to provide the electricity for lighting, cooking an so on—all to keep you chaps nice and comfortable," the mate said in a cultured English accent.

"I apologize, as it's a bit warm down here," he continued. That was no exaggeration, as it must have been in the 90s. Rows of iron doors, leading to huge fireboxes, were fed by dozens of men stripped to the waist, shoveling coal. "I'm glad

I don't have to do that job," thought Jed. He realized how lucky he was to be doing something he loved—riding and working on motorcycles. They soon vacated the boiler room to see the engine rooms. Large piston engines, several stories in height, turned the huge propeller shafts. These were maintained by mechanics, seen on stairs and catwalks around the machinery keeping everything oiled and adjusted. Unlike the boiler rooms, black with coal dust, the engine rooms were spotless. Jed marveled not only at the size of these various engine components, but could hardly imagine what size of machine tools the ship's builders, John Brown and Co. of Clydebank had at their disposal. And he thought motorcycles and their manufacture was complicated.

Moving upwards several decks, they entered the kitchens where dozens of chefs, cooks, dishwashers and various helpers were toiling over stoves and preparation tables. "Our menus are equal or better than that of the Ritz," said the mate with pride. "Our head chef was trained in France, as were most of our sous-chefs." Again, the size of everything was remarkable. Huge coffee percolators held 100 or more gallons each, Jed estimated. Adjacent to the kitchens were massive food lockers containing whole beef carcasses, fresh produce and all manner of foodstuffs. There were also separate rooms containing various liquors and what the mate described as the finest wine cellar afloat.

Next on the list was a tour of the various classes of accommodation. "Steerage" was first on the list. These tiny quarters were sparsely populated on this voyage, but the officer explained it would be packed on the return with immigrants coming to America. "They are quite a mixed assortment," said the officer. "They come from all over: Jews, Russians, Ukrainians and those Irish that are always fighting. I really don't know what you chaps do with them. You should hear the commotion they make when they first see that Statue of Liberty thing you have in New York harbor." Working upwards in style from steerage through third, second, and finally approaching first class, the mate wished them well, apologizing to Jake, who was not allowed on the first—class deck. "We will see you two," he said quietly aside to Jed and George, "at the Captain's table this evening." Jed and George promised to get Jake after dinner that evening, and smuggle him into the first class lounge. Jake had brought a tuxedo for the occasion.

On the way back to their staterooms, the two first-class passengers passed dowagers and aging gentlemen "taking the airs" on deck chairs. There were more active types playing tennis and various shipboard games on the first-class deck, as the weather was sunny and warm, a bit unusual on the Atlantic. It was to be a smooth crossing.

After dressing for dinner, Jed and George, suitably attired, headed for the first-class lounge and dining room, where cocktails would be served. The dining room had a ceiling three stories in height, featuring a huge crystal chandelier. Access was through impressive cut-glass French doors. The décor was baroque with rare wood paneling and lots of flamboyant art objects in view. Waiters circulated with trays of fine French Champagne and hors-d'oeurves. Liquid refreshments stimulated conversation, and after an hour of socializing, the guests were seated at tables. Jed and George, as promised, were seated at the Captain's table. There they enjoyed an excellent meal accompanied by a selection of fine wines. The captain assured his guests that the crossing would indeed be smooth and asked if all was well. Jed thought that it was probably the most elegant evening his life.

After Dinner, Jed and George called on Jake, and then led him up to the first class deck. The seaman who was keeping the riff-raff from climbing above their station stepped aside with a smile upon receiving a ten-pound note from George. Jake slipped into the crowd unnoticed and was soon socializing with George and Jed's new friends in the first-class lounge. As they stood at the bar, an English Lord who had been at their table at dinner remarked, "I say, Cunard is letting the side down. They've actually let a fuzzy-wuzzy into our lounge. He must be an American."

"Indeed he is," said George forcing a smile. "His name is Scott Joplin. You ought to hear him tinkle the ivories!" As if on cue, Joplin strolled over to the grand piano and, flicking back the tails of his waistcoat with a flourish like a concert pianist, sat down and launched into the Maple Leaf Rag. An hour-long medley of Joplin's playing soon erased any feelings of racism: even the British Lord was tapping his feet to the rhythm, and was later seen with his arm around Joplin congratulating him. The music was infectious.

During the evening, the three friends noticed two young ladies in the company of one about ten years older. They turned out to be two English sisters, accompanied by their governess, returning to England after a "grand tour," around the world. George announced that he would see what he could do to disarm the governess so the boys could chase the two younger ladies. The suave uncle soon had the governess charmed, while Jed and Jake were telling the girls of their great exploits on the board tracks. Jake merely told the truth, but Jed embellished his racing career. Later in the evening, George disappeared with the governess. Shortly thereafter Jed wandered off to his room with one of the young girls. The other girl was gaga over the handsome, debonair Jake, until she learned he was in second class. She instantly turned frosty, as there was no way she was going below stairs with a second-class passenger. The class system was very much alive amongst the British.

For the rest of the voyage, George and Jed hardly surfaced, spending much time in their staterooms with the English ladies. Jake, meanwhile, spent his waking hours jogging on the second-class deck and doing calisthenics in his smaller stateroom. He was, after all, a professional racer, determined to keep himself in shape, in contrast to his friend Fireball, who was far more interested in drink and loose women than in maintaining his physical self.

On arrival in Liverpool, the three companions went through customs and checked to see that the motorcycles had cleared. There was one to be ridden by Jake, three more to be ridden by Billy Well's three local riders, a spare road racer and #21. Wells was to have standard road bikes available as well for transportation on the Island. Upon customs clearance, they met Wells, a tall, debonair Englishman dressed in jodhpurs and leather boots, sporting a stylish trilby cap. He escorted them by carriage, with four racers and parts following by wagon to a nearby dock. This is where they would load the bikes on board the Isle of Man, *Steam Packet*, to Douglas. They loaded #21, and one of the racers, in a separate carriage to travel to London, where Jake was entered in the London-to-Edinburgh Road Trial.

Racing on public roads had been outlawed in England early in the century, largely due to the carnage created by such racing on the continent. Crowds of spectators got in the way of the racing machines, where many were killed, mostly by the large racing cars. Events such as the London-to-Edinburgh trial were, of necessity, timed events. Although, strictly speaking, not a race, a trial often ended up as such. The trial began the day after their arrival in Liverpool, so there was barely time to hop the train for London before the event began.

After a fitful sleep, George and Jed saw the bikes off in the London-to-Edinburgh. Jake's Red Indian stood out in the crowd, attracting a lot of attention with its chain drive and two-speed gearbox. One very tall rider approached Jake and introduced himself as Oily Karslake. Oily was riding a machine that he had built in 1901, which had a De Dion engine, similar to the Orient that Jed had received on his birthday in 1900. Evidently the engine had been rescued from a 19th century tricycle! It was highly modified, with a two-speed NSU gear added, as well as a three-speed Sturmey Archer hub and had an extra exhaust port added to the engine. Built into a very early BAT frame, it was tall and ungainly, not unlike its rider. Nevertheless the three visitors were to learn that Oily was one of England's greatest trials riders. His machine was christened *The Dreadnought*.

Also present was Charlie Collier, standing beside his Matchless V-twin. This machine looked like a worthy opponent to the little Indian. Jed was reminded of that first road trial he had been in, the Boston to New York in 1903. It was there that he had met Oscar Hedstrom and George Hendee, along with other notables, who had since done well in the USA. Although he did not realize it at the time, Jed was rubbing shoulders with others who were equally well known in their native England. He spent about 30 minutes discussing trials-type riding with a young gentleman by the name of George Brough, who was riding one of his father's products, a Brough with an opposed twin engine similar to those fitted to several Douglas machines also entered in the trials. These flat, twin engines were ticking over very smoothly, without the noise of the various singles and V-Twins. Jed was particularly impressed with the big twin J.A.P. powered NUT and BAT, also entered, although he felt the belt drive was a bit primitive compared to the chains on Jake's Indian. The weather was overcast: if it rained, he realized, Jake would have an advantage, just like the Indians had had over his Orient in 1903. Soon the riders were off, and George and Jed joined Billy Wells in a first-class compartment en route to Edinburgh, for the finish.

The train was much smaller than those that George and Jed were used to, but it was well appointed. Time passed pleasantly with Wells laying out for the two Americans his proposal regarding the marketing of Indians in England. The British motorcycle industry was very large and, like the US, there were many brands, most of which were assembled jobs using proprietary parts from manufacturers such as JAP, Precision, and so forth. And like American machines, nearly all used German-made Bosch magnetos. Speedometers, where fitted, appeared to be all of US manufacture. Carburetors were mostly of the "two lever" variety. The British showed a preference for vertical throttle slides, as opposed to the butterfly type commonly used in American carburetors. Fireball noted all of these particulars, storing as much information as he could for possible future use.

Pleasantly refreshed after their train ride, with brandy and cigars compliments of George, the three awaited the riders at the finish. It had been a wet trip for the riders: in first place there was a triumphant, but muddy, Jake DeRosier, who, with a perfect score, won a gold medal. It was his first accomplishment abroad; he received enthusiastic applause from an admiring British and Scottish crowd of motorcycle enthusiasts lining the route. Billy Wells, dreaming of great Indian sales, was ecstatic. Oily Karslake also placed well with the ancient Dreadnought He also scored a gold medal, as did Charlie Collier.

"These fellows are great sportsmen, Fireball," said Jake. "Charlie Collier lost a few points by stopping to help me with a tire puncture. You know how hopeless I am with those things. It was a good thing he was handy, as you were no doubt on that train drinking Scotch." Jed smiled at his friend. "Actually it was brandy from France called Cognac. It is pretty good stuff. I have a bottle for your trip back to Liverpool." After celebrating with Jake's bottle, and a short night's sleep, they were on another train to Liverpool, where they were to board the Isle of Man Steam Packet to "Mona's Isle".

In the sheds, waiting for the Steam Packet to board, were more motorcycles than Jed had ever seen in one place, even on the Indian shipping floor. Not only the race bikes that were being transported there, but all manner of road-going machines, as well with their riders, were packed together. A profusion of new names decorated the tanks: Humber, Zenith, Kerry, James, Douglas, Beardmore Precision, Premier, Aldays and Onions, B.A.T., N.U.T., Rudge, Bradbury, and FN, to name but a few. Most were single-cylinder machines, but a few were big twins, such as the big N.U.T., which, as the owner pointed out, had an overhead-valve *90 bore* J.A.P. engine. The FN had four cylinders in-line, as did a magnificent, green, two-wheeled conveyance with a steering wheel, bearing the name Wilkinson. The owner explained that his Wilkinson was built by the famous sword company.

Jed began a conversation with a rider next to him in the shed, who was on an older machine with a stylish cane-work sidecar. "I'm R.F. Baker from Yew Tree Farm, up Newbury way," said the gentleman. "The bike is a 1905 Riley, which I have updated with one of the new Sturmey Archer three-speed hubs." Jed examined the hub with some amazement. According to Baker, a three-speed gear, as well as a clutch, had been fitted into the rear hub, which could not have been more than six-inches in diameter. Thought Jed "One more gear than our Indians. Maybe it will be more difficult to win over here than Mr. Hedstrom seems to think." Jed further learned that Baker had fitted the 1910 Mills and Fulford sidecar to take his wife on their honeymoon to France. The customs plate was still attached to the handlebars.

"Percy Riley invented and patented the concept of valve overlap," explained Baker. "This allows the engine to breathe, clearing out the spent gasses from the combustion chamber, and filling it with a rich, clean, explosive charge. Obviously, you need mechanically operated intake valves to do this. It's strange that so many manufacturers are sticking to those old naturally aspirated systems." When the ship was ready to load, Baker depressed the rocking clutch pedal to disengage the back wheel, and then simply pedaled the stationary machine to start the engine. No running or pushing required.

"Now that is pretty slick," commented Jed to his companions.

Just before departure, the crew strapped down the motorcycles and related gear. The three soon learned, to their discomfort, the reason for this precaution. The relatively short trip across the Irish Sea to the Isle of Man was far rougher than their trans-Atlantic voyage had been. Upon arrival in Douglas, several hours later, they were rather green. George had lost the contents of his stomach to the sharks. It was good to be once again on *terra Firma*. Billy Wells, on the other hand, appeared chipper and seemingly unaffected by it all.

"Moorehouse at TT"

Billy Wells soon introduced them to his local riders. "Meet the great Jake De Rosier," said Billy to his three hopefuls. They were obviously in awe of Jake who was famous in Indian circles. Oliver Godfrey was a small man with a ready smile, while Arthur Moorhouse, the other Englishman, was tall and rather serious looking. Charles Franklin, the Irish rider, proved to be the most technically knowledgeable of the entire group present. He and Jed were soon deep in conversation concerning valve overlap and other related topics. Franklin was intrigued by Jed's descriptions of the ported cylinders used on some of the board track machines.

"Oliver Godfrey at TT"

"I wonder . . . do you suppose that in expelling the spent gases, and creating a vacuum to bring in the fresh charge, that that's what is giving you the extra power? If that's the case, it's the same as Percy Riley's valve overlap. Perhaps you colonials are in violation of his patent." smiled Franklin. "I'll bet its spectacular for the spectators, particularly at dusk, as I understand you run in the evening. I don't think I'd fancy those slivers." At that point Fireball removed his shirt to show the group his many and various scars. Jake, on the other hand, had no such wounds, as he had not fallen off his motorcycle like his friend Fireball.

"Charles Franklin at TT"

"There is enough time for several days of practice," explained Wells to the Americans. "Racing on public roads has been banned in most of Europe now, as a result of the carnage created by the huge racing cars. People used to line the way to watch Panhards, Napiers, Atalas, etc., and didn't know enough to keep out of the way when things went amiss. There were quite a few casualties. Our friends on the Isle of Man have taken a much more liberal approach to it all. So there we are. They do have a few simple rules, so please obey them. During practice, the machines must be equipped with silencers, and there will be no use of exhaust cutouts. You will notice that the bikes also come with long straight pipes. These can be fitted during the actual race. The rules state that the exhaust outlet has to exit at the rear axle or further back, so we can't run the short dumper pipes you use in America on the board tracks. Also, ported cylinders are forbidden for the same reasons. I suggest we get at it as soon as you have rested and refreshed yourselves after your travels. Thanks for coming, Fireball. Oscar Hedstrom spoke highly of you, and we'd appreciate any assistance you can give. Thank you, also, George, for escorting the lads. I assume you kept them from temptations during the voyage." George smiled and nodded in amused agreement.

The following morning, after a breakfast that included Manx kippers, fried bread, blood pudding and other greasy delicacies, the boys were out on the course, preparing the race bikes. Jed felt as though he was back on the Steam Packet again, until the greasy meal made it through the first part of his digestive system. All was well afterwards, and they were all anxious to start the TT.

Fireball made his way through the pits, surveying the competition. The Scott team arrived from Ramsay with their two-stroke twins. *Two strokes* in America were considered somewhat sub-standard, but these Scotts were different. All the Scott riders wore purple leathers to match the paint on their "biscuit tin" petrol tanks. By comparison, the Scott machines were tiny, with step-through frames like a lady's bike, but something told Fireball they would be a force to be reckoned with, given their water-cooling, twin cylinders, rotary valves and, obviously, light weight. He met a Scott rider by the name of Frank Appleby, who was, as it turned out, a partner of Well's man, Oliver Godfrey. The two of them owned a motorcycle shop selling both Scotts and Indians.

The Rudge team was another well-represented group with much factory support. The Rudges were single-speed one-lungers, but despite their light weight, Jed figured the Indian two—speeders would have the advantage on the course, which, by all accounts, was quite hilly and twisty. The Triumph team was also well represented. Although they had the three-speed Sturmey Archer hubs he'd seen on the Riley, he considered that the Indian twins were superior in speed and endurance. The proof would be in the pudding.

At 9:00 AM the bikes were ready for the "off" as they began to circulate the 36-mile circuit. Jed took an Indian supplied by Billy Wells—a "little twin" single speeder. Using a map supplied by Wells, Jed traveled on back roads to various parts of the TT course to survey the progress of his friend Jake. He was aware of how intimidating the TT course would be to Jake.

Corners were blind in both directions. Further, the roads changed in elevation, while the route took the racers through villages with stone walls and buildings very close to the race line. As he moved about the course, Jed observed Jake wowing the British and Manx crowds with his spectacular foot sliding left-hand drifts.

On the right-handers, Jake was less in control, braking either too soon or too late. After all, Jake was accustomed to racing with no brakes at all. By the end of the first day, Jake had fallen off three times, but had set a new lap record. The great man was beginning to become somewhat rattled, which was a new thing to his friend Jed. Meanwhile, Godfrey, Franklin, and Moorehouse circulated the course at a steady pace—well into the top few riders' times. Obviously road racing was an entirely different kettle of fish compared to board racing. Jed tried to keep pace with his friend De Rosier, traveling inside the circle on back roads, but it was impossible on that 36 mile course. He was unable to help apart from moral support at the end of the day. Jed had the little Indian at his disposal, while George joined him on a three-speed Triumph, which he had rented from a Manxman. Truth be known, the two of them spent more time sampling the local Manx bitter than supporting Jake's efforts. By the end of the practice period, poor Jake had crashed a total of six times, ruining two pairs of his trademark ballet tights. The third pair were well patched and sewn up.

On race day morning, Jed was in the Indian pits, helping to fit fresh tires on the racers, topping up oil, and fitting the long swept-back straight pipes. George wandered about, cigar in hand, offering free advice to anyone who would listen.

At intervals of one minute, the racers started. After the first ten or so, very few spectators, apart from the Manx Boy Scouts, who kept track, were able to tell who was in the lead. Jed and George took off on their bikes, trying to catch the action at various points along the course. Sitting at Kate's Cottage, with pints of the Island's finest at hand, George and Jed spotted Frank Phillip's Scott screaming by at a great rate of speed. They later learned that Phillip had set the fastest lap of the Senior at 50.11 mph., no mean feat on those windy, undulated, gravel roads. Unfortunately for Phillip, the tapered shaft and nut holding the rotary valve came loose, rendering him a non-finisher. All the Scotts had similar problems, with Frank Appleby the only Scott finisher. He had to tighten the rotary valve several times during the race and finished dead last. Meanwhile George and Jed were sampling another pint at Glen Helen, when they witnessed Vic Surridge crash his Rudge. He had made a sterling effort, pressing his single-speed, belt-drive Rudge to its very limit. He was chasing the two-speed bikes when he misjudged a turn, crashing into a stone wall. Unfortunately, Vic's injuries proved fatal, making him the first fatality in TT history.

Oliver Godfrey was much in the lead at this time, constantly swapping places with Charlie Collier, riding one of his V-twin Matchless machines. Collier had won this race before, and was determined to repeat the feat. They were both shadowed closely by Franklin and Moorhouse, both riding Wells' Indians. As they crossed the finish line, it was Godfrey, Collier, Franklin, and Moorhouse. Harry Collier, Charlie's brother, was right behind them riding another Matchless. The

Indian team made an immediate protest, claiming that Charlie Collier had made an unscheduled fuel stop. As it turned out, he had. As the TT was supposed to be a "tourist trophy" race, fuel was limited by the rules, so Collier was disqualified. Godfrey's average speed over the course was over 49 mph. Indian bikes, therefore, had won a sweep: first, second and third. This proved to be the only American win in TT history. Indian also managed to save the TT. With Vic Surridge's fatality, the organizers wished to shut down the TT races. They could not, however, as it would leave the Americans as the last victors. Britain had to redeem herself, so the Isle of Man TT survives to this day.

Jake De Rosier finished a barely credible 16th, but was disqualified for accepting outside help. Fireball had repaired a tire for the mechanically inept Jake when he happened to have a flat opposite the pub where Jed and George were sipping beer on the porch. After his painful crashes, and riding in a totally new discipline, his accomplishment was quite amazing. Jake was not used to losing though, and Jed noticed that the fire had gone out of his eyes. Before the week was out, and feeling somewhat second class, Jake decided to challenge Charlie Collier to a series of match races at the Brooklands racetrack in Weybridge, west of London. Collier readily accepted, unaware that this was a personal challenge made without authorization by the Indian factory or, more importantly, Oscar Hedstrom. In fact Hedstrom had specifically instructed them to head back to the USA if they were fortunate to win the TT. As the TT was the main target, Oscar felt they should quit while they were ahead, and not risk being beaten at Brooklands. Jed understood fully that his somewhat cushy little job of supporting Jake was at stake. Jake De Rosier, nevertheless, was determined to press ahead. He yearned for vindication—a victory over the local favorite, their racing hero.

Brooklands Racetrack, conceived in 1906, opened in 1907. With racing on public roads prohibited in England, motor vehicle suppliers believed that a high-speed circuit was needed to demonstrate and test their products. The Brooklands 2-¾ mile concrete oval was used for motorcycle as well as car racing. It featured a "test hill" leading from one of the straight-aways, which was used for hill climbing. The concrete had been spread in panels. At the time, this was a new type of construction process; little was known of structure, expansion and contraction of this relatively new building material. This method resulted in a very rough surface. The problem may have been complicated further by the monster cars that regularly ran there, such as the Fiats, which had displacements of up to 28 liters, or 1708 cubic inches. As Fireball said to Jake, "Well at least if you fall off here, you won't get any slivers. I'm glad we shortened the front spring in old #21 though. It would have broken for sure." Jed was well aware that if the front spring were to break on an Indian, the wheel could suddenly lock up, projecting the rider forward.

"Jake DeRosier at Brooklands"

Brooklands was also the home of Britain's fledgling aircraft industry, so the Americans were treated to the sights and sounds of A.V. Roe's flying machines, when they arrived at the track on July 8th, a week prior to the match races. Going onto the track alone with #21, Jake set three new word records: I kilometer at 85.32 mph; 1 mile at 87.38 mph; and 5 miles at an average speed of 80.72 mph. Not a bad start on the concrete!

On July 15th large crowds gathered to see who had the fastest machine, their hero, Charlie Collier or the flashy American, Jake De Rosier. As expected the crowd roared their approval as Charlie Collier took the lead over the first two laps of 5 ½ miles; in fact the Matchless led for most of the race with Jake drafting closely behind. To everyone's complete surprise, De Rosier pulled out towards the finish, winning by a convincing machine length.

The second race consisted of five laps, or 13-½ miles. Jake again chose the drafting strategy, but had a blowout in the third lap. While he was able to ride it out without crashing, Charlie won easily. The third event was a long, ten-lapper, 27-¼ miles. Jake's machine failed to start due to a broken magneto lead. Once resolved, the race got under way. While Jake led by a wheel length on the first lap, the second was all Charlie's. On the third, Collier was really forging ahead when his ignition cut out: the severe vibration had cut the switch. By the time Charlie managed to reconnect it and restart the Matchless, Jake was well beyond reach. Until that incident, the rated speed for the Matchless was much faster than the Indian.

The results were:

Race #1: 2 laps (5 ½ miles)
First: Jake De Rosier, 80.59 mph
Second: Charlie Collier, 80.53 mph

Race #2: 5 laps (13 ½ miles)
First: Charlie Collier, 79.92 mph
Second: Jake De Rosier, DNF

Race #3: 10 laps (27 miles)
First: Jake De Rosier, 78.64 mph
Second: Charlie Collier, 77.4 mph.

Fireball let out a long sigh of relief. Luck was with them, he thought. It could have gone either way. It could have been disastrous in more ways than one.

On the day before the departure from England, Jake ran # 21 again at Brooklands, again raising his speed records: the kilometer at 88.7 mph, and the mile at 88.23 mph. At the end of the day, the Colliers put on a grand banquet in Jake's honor. It was an immensely satisfying conclusion to the trip.

Charlie Collier had developed a friendship with the Indian team during the various races, particularly with Jake, whom he admired immensely. The feeling was mutual. Charlie and his brother, Harry, were two of the greatest motorcycle racers in England. Together, they more or less dominated the Isle of Man races from the beginning. The Matchless Motorcycle Works, in Plumstead, began with the manufacturing of bicycles by Harry Collier, father of Charlie and Harry junior. The elder Collier also attended the banquet. Beginning with bicycles, Charlie had been a cycling champion in 1899 at the age of 14. With racing on public roads banned in England, as in America, early motorcycle racing began on existing bicycle tracks. The two brothers from Plumstead were fortunate to have several close to their home. Crystal Palace, Canning Town and the Stadium all provided venues for them to hone their skills. Charlie won his first motorcycle race in 1901 covering five miles in 5 minutes: 54 seconds, on one of his father's creations. Again in 1904, Charlie won a five-mile race at the Crystal Palace, defeating J.F. Crundall, riding a chain-drive Humber.

The H. Collier and Sons Ltd.'s Matchless Motorcycle was typical of many of England's many small manufacturer's products. Frames were built in-house, but engines and various other mechanical components supplied by various manufactures, near and far. Engines often came from the Continent, originally from de Dion Bouton, and Givaudan, and later from London's J.A.P. factory. The Colliers spent not a penny on fancy advertising. Instead, they let the race successes of their "Matchless in Name and Reputation" machines tell the tale.

At the banquet, Charlie told the three Americans the history of the TT races. The first race on the Island took place in 1905 in conjunction with auto races held there annually. The initial route was triangular in design, taking in the towns of Douglas, Ballacraine and Castletown. The roads were extremely rough and the rules stated the machines were to have an all-up weight of just 110 pounds or less. Consequently, the bikes were very spindly. As a result, only seven of the original seventeen entries survived the race trials. While many saw it as a bit of a farce, the Collier brothers were proud to be among the surviving seven, especially with Charlie finishing second.

The following year, when it was not possible to co-ordinate the race with the automobiles, the Auto Cycle Club developed their own Tourist Trophy races for motorcycles in 1907, and the famous TT was born. Instead of using the unrealistic weight restrictions of the 1905 race, they placed a limit on fuel consumption. It was this ruling which was to cause Charlie's disqualification in the 1911 event for stopping at an unscheduled fuel stop.

At the first TT, seventeen *singles*, and eight *twins* lined up at the starting line. Among them were the Collier brothers riding 3-½ hp JAP-powered singles. Harry won with an average speed of 38.5 mph and a recorded fuel mileage of 94.5 mph. Interestingly, Billy Wells rode in the twin cylinder race on a Vindec, and Oliver Godfrey rode a Rex. Charlie Franklin rode a Humber in the single-cylinder race along with the Colliers. As the singles proved faster than the twins, the twins were given an 80 cc advantage when the two classes were combined in the longer 1911 race. Mechanically operated intake valves soon put an end to the single cylinder's advantage. The original magnificent Tourist Trophy, donated by Marquis de Mouzilly St Mars, was awarded to Charlie, its first winner. All later trophies were replicas. Harry won the Senior race in 1909, recording the fastest lap of 52.27 mph.

Charlie Collier had been a formidable competitor for Jake. While he had proven himself the better man in the TT, Jake had redeemed himself at Brooklands. Jed was pleased to notice that the old sparkle had returned to his friend's eyes.

To Charlie, Jake said, "You should bring that Matchless to America and see if you can take me on the boards."

"I'd love to have a go, Jake," Charlie replied, "but I think you would shellac me good! Anyway, I think Harry Senior would sack me if I left. Also, I wouldn't like a back full of sliver scars like your chum Fireball here. Lets keep in touch, though. It has really been jolly good fun getting to know you." With that, they all shook hands. The Americans, rather the worse for wear as a result of strong drink, returned to their hotel to prepare for their return to the States. The Lusitania set sail the following morning.

The return trip on the Lusitania was smooth sailing in most respects. Jake was more upbeat after his success at Brooklands, but didn't talk much about the TT. His lack of success there obviously bothered him. George and Fireball drank and caroused in the first-class lounges, while Jake remained in his second-class accommodations. Unfortunately for the first-class passengers, there were no young ladies with governesses to take advantage of on the return voyage.

As New York skyline began to emerge from the fog, George and Jed watching from the first-class deck, looked down on the swarm of immigrants below crowding to the prow.

"There she is!" yelled a man with an Irish accent as the Statue of Liberty came into view. With that, they all became animated and began to sing and dance.

"It happens every time," sneered a crewman standing beside George and Jed, "They think they've arrived in heaven, for Christ's sake."

CHAPTER THIRTEEN

INDIAN'S GOLDEN ERA

Jed and Jake said their goodbyes to George at the train station, before boarding their train back to the Indian factory in Springfield and their company responsibilities. As both men were anxious to see what was developing on the board track scene during their absence, they went immediately to the experimental department, Jed's usual domain when he wasn't traveling with Jake. There were two newly designed machines sitting on builder's benches. They looked like the regular race machines, but differed in that the crankcases were larger in diameter, and the barrels and heads were more robust. To top it all off, they had four overhead valves in each cylinder. These were the first two 8-valve Indians ever built. Jake was visibly excited, more than Jed had seen him since they left for England. He rushed off to Oscar Hedstrom's office, leaving Jed to examine the bikes. Jed fully understood that Indian had certainly developed something truly special.

As he was imagining himself on one of these magnificent 8-valve motorcycles, Jed's train of thought was interrupted by loud, angry voices coming from Hedstrom's office. He ambled casually in that direction and stuck his ear to the door, hoping to avoid detection by any other employees.

"You are a has-been, Jake! Why the hell should I let you have one of those new machines when young guys like Eddie Hasha and Ray Seymour can probably ride circles around you. I can't believe it. Sixteenth in the TT and then, on top of it all, getting disqualified. Hell, I could have done better myself and I haven't raced for years," hollered Oscar. "Billy Wells must be having a good laugh at our expense with his three boys coming 1,2,3, and our great star, De Rosier, doing so poorly!"

"You forgot I won the match races at Brooklands," yelled Jake.

"Big deal," replied Hedstrom. "Any idiot could have done that with the faster Indian on that huge concrete oval. All you had to do was sit there and cruise around."

"Collier's Matchless is every bit as fast," retorted Jake. "Also try holding onto a machine while it's bucking around on that rough concrete, particularly with a couple of broken ribs like I have, by gar. If you don't give me one of those eight valves to ride, I will quit."

"There's the door. Help yourself," said Hedstrom. "Bloody frog," he muttered under his breath.

Jed stepped deftly aside as Jake stormed out of the office, slamming the door behind him. Jed said to the red-faced Jake, "I don't think I am officially back to work until tomorrow. I think we should adjourn to the tavern where you can buy me a beer and explain what your plans are now. I hope I can keep my job."

As they hoisted a few across the road, Jake having more than usual, Jake decided to take the train to Chicago, where he would offer his services to Mr. Schwinn. The Excelsior factory had good racing equipment; in the past Schwinn had approached Jake. Jed decided to remain with Indian if he could keep his job He made a mental note to befriend Hasha and Seymour. Maybe the boys liked good-looking ladies such as Lucy and her friends. Jed was willing to share and had the keen instincts of a survivor.

The following day, Oscar Hedstrom approached Jed in the experimental dept. He put his arm around Jed and said, "Your friend Jake De Rosier has left us, I'm afraid, Fireball. I would like you to stay with us if you will. Billy Wells has cabled to say what a help you were in their efforts on the Island and elsewhere, and what a splendid fellow your uncle is. You obviously have a good family behind you. If you could stick with us, and help with the race team, we certainly would appreciate it. Having your own rail pass from your uncle certainly is a bonus. You can also have the odd track ride, which I know you enjoy."

Jed really hadn't been much help on the overseas trip. He decided he had better thank his uncle George for supplying all that good booze for Billy and his friends as well as that delightful evening they had all enjoyed at that London bawdy house, compliments of George. His uncle's strong influence was indispensable in making Jed a survivor.

CHAPTER FOURTEEN

MOTORDROMES OR *MURDERDROMES*

Board tracks were springing up all over the country, all built by Jack Prince with help from his right hand man Paul, "Daredevil," Derkum. While Jake De Rosier managed to get on the Excelsior team, he didn't do as well as he had at Indian. Perhaps, as Hedstrom had suggested, he was indeed past his prime.

With the additional tracks, came additional accidents and carnage. "Neck and Neck with Death," read the sign outside the Detroit Michigan Motordrome. Fireball traveled with the Indian riders, providing mechanical assistance and riding his own machine as a privateer. He developed a new skill, using an old Indian single he had acquired: he learned how to ride while standing on his head on the saddle facing backwards. This, and other tricks, amused the crowds at half-time in the infield. One of his most lucrative ventures came when he overheard some spectators saying, "I bet that the Excelsior will win," or "I'll bet Hasha passes Albright in the next lap." Jed would make that eventuality entirely possible.

Jed became a bookie. As Lucy had done fairly well with her little business, they pooled their resources. Lucy put up some money to cover Jed's bets. His involvement with Lucy naturally led to another venture, which was that of pimping. While in the Los Angeles Area, he became Lucy's marketing department. She had bought a house, and had become the youngest madam in the Los Angeles Basin. This provided him with a place to stay while in the area—his favorite "hotel." It came with a butler, an excellent cook, a good wine cellar and about twenty young ladies to entertain paying guests.

At the new Los Angeles Stadium in Feb 1912, Jed watched as his old friend Jake De Rosier rode his factory Excelsior. He finished second behind Joe Walters, but ahead of Charlie Balke. The new Big-Valve Excelsiors were very fast, becoming a threat to the Indians. One week later, De Rosier and Balke, fierce competitors although on the same team, collided on the track. Unfortunately, the resulting injuries would eventually take Jake's life, but not before his savings and winnings were exhausted on health care. In 1913, at the age of thirty-three, with an amazing nine hundred victories, Jake succumbed to his considerable injuries.

"Clever tricks"

Jake's funeral procession slowly wound through his hometown of Springfield. As the procession passed the Indian factory, the employees lining the street removed their hats and stood quietly, a silent salute to a great rider. Jake had been barred from the factory grounds since his fierce blowup with Oscar Hedstrom. Nevertheless, on this day the tools were laid down, while the machinery stood idle.

From an upper floor window, an unseen hand parted the curtains to allow an unobstructed view. It was Hedstom himself who had ordered the factory closed. And it was from his pocket alone that the expenses for the lavish funeral were paid.

Jed was spending most of his time in the east now. Most major cities had board tracks as board track racing was at the height of its popularity. Jed was still racing at the back of the pack and doing his crowd-pleasing stunts. It was at the new Speed Bowl in Newark, New Jersey, where Jed witnessed the worst board track accident of all time. This was to portend the beginning of the end of this motor sport.

The Indian team had decided to see a picture show on the evening of September 8th, the night before the races. Jed had become friendly with Eddy Hasha. Although he had originally sought out Hasha for selfish reasons, he quite enjoyed the man's company. Hasha was a married man with no time for the drinking or loose women favored by Jed. Nevertheless they got on well enough. During the film, Eddie blacked out. He later admitted to Jed that for a while he could not see the screen, but later felt fine.

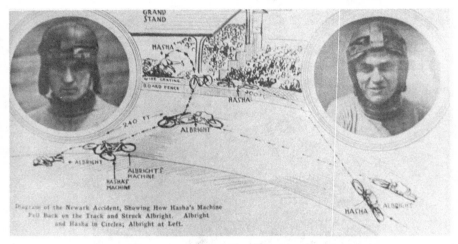

Program of the Newark Accident, Showing How Hasha's Machine Fell Back on the Track and Struck Albright. Albright and Hasha in Circles; Albright at Left.

"Bad Press"

In the final event of the following day, while Eddy Hasha and Ray Seymour were running scratch, Roy Peck and Johnnie Albright were given a quarter lap advantage, and Frank and Johnnie King another quarter. On the third lap, Eddie was lapping Fireball with Seymour ahead. Peck, Albright, and the King brothers were hot on his heels. As Fireball looked up high on the banking above, he saw Hasha reach down to adjust his carburetor. He picked up speed, but suddenly shot out, colliding with the top rail. Four boys, leaning over the rail, were struck by the errant machine, which also took out Albright's bike. The boys were decapitated. The rear wheel of Hasha's machine flew into the crowd, killing another spectator before crashing to the infield where it killed yet another spectator. Hasha and Albright later succumbed to their injuries, bringing the total fatalities to eight. Fireball rolled to a stop, surveyed the carnage, and immediately threw up. It was to be his last ride on the boards.

"Hasha and Albright's Indians"

State authorities immediately shut down the Newark track. It never re-opened. Board track racing fell out of favor over the next few years: their detractors referred to these facilities as "Murderdromes."

CHAPTER FIFTEEN

FIREBALL'S LAST DAYS AT INDIAN

Although Jed still followed the race team from place to place, he was becoming more interested in his job at the factory. He worked on the new developments in the experimental department, which included the new spring-cradle frame featured on the road models in 1913. He tried one of the first and was amazed at the added comfort. He could have made it coast to coast much faster if he'd had one of these six years ago when he rode the Harley. The progress was amazing. The big surprise came in 1914, when George Hendee decided the company needed a new top-of-the-line model. He christened it the *Hendee Special*. Cadillac had pioneered electric starting in 1913; George Hendee decided his motorcycle would have one too. The electrical factory that developed Cadillac's starter happened to be in Springfield. Hendee contacted with this company to adapt the system to a motorcycle. The method called for two six-volt batteries, mounted on each side. When the starter was activated, the batteries, connected in series spun the engine with twelve volts of power. Once started, the rider was to release the lever. The effect was to switch the batteries to a parallel connection, allowing the starter generator to be charged while putting out a 6-volt current. The battery system made it possible to have electric lighting, horn and ignition, making the magneto redundant.

While Jed was very taken with the gadgetry of the Hendee Special, factory rumor was that Oscar Hedstrom was less than impressed with the concept. As the first models hit the streets, Jed began to appreciate Hedstrom's reservations, especially as it was he who would be summoned by unhappy dealers to cure problems.

The vibration of the motorcycle, combined with the rough roads of the day played havoc with the batteries, causing riders to become stranded. The plates in the batteries shook loose and shorted out, leaving riders without ignition. The second version of the Hendee Special was fitted with a magneto, mounted higher and to the right to clear the 20 lb starter. At least a stranded rider could push start the bike and get home. This was still not a satisfactory solution: a third version was fitted with a kick starter as well as the magneto. Even this belt-and-braces approach proved unsatisfactory, as battery failure affected the lighting as well. After just two hundred machines were sold, the Hendee Specials were withdrawn from production. Dealers were forced to remove the starters and make partial refunds to disgruntled owners. The loss of confidence in Indian over this issue proved to be the first mistake of the world's largest motorcycle company. It was to be the beginning of a slow, downward slide from its best ever year of 1913.

Oscar Hedstrom announced his retirement after the Hendee Special debacle. Jed could detect an unmistakable strain between the two founders during Hedstom's retirement party. The following day he was summoned into Hendee's office.

"Your protector has gone, Fireball. You may have fooled him all these years, but I can see through you. You're not only a shiftless bum at heart, but I know full well you take strong drink often and to excess—and you consort with loose women. You're fired!"

When Jed's request for a reference was met with a stony silence, he went to the office and picked up his pay packet. He noticed with some relief that there was enough in it to finance a good afternoon across at the tavern. It was, in fact, opening time.

As he recovered from his hangover the following day, and after the departure of his unscheduled overnight female guest, Jed decided to travel to Chicago to try his luck at Schwinn. He was hoping that Jake might have told the old man what a good fellow he was. Jed knew he could probably get a job at Harley Davidson, knowing Bill and Arthur, but decided to do that as a last resort only. He didn't want to risk meeting up with his past in the Milwaukee area. He had run into Mabel while racing in Milwaukee. She showed up at the track with a little boy at her side. Jed knew this boy was his. She was now married to Harold Wilson's youngest son, who she had in tow. The slow-witted man bore no ill will towards Jed, while the little boy clung to Jed's leg in admiration, captivated by the excitement around the track. Jed had no desire to repeat that uncomfortable experience.

CHAPTER SIXTEEN

FIREBALL HIRED AT EXCELSIOR

Ignatz Shwinn led off. "Jake told me all about you, Fireball," he said as he welcomed Jed into his Chicago office, "I really miss that boy. He had a great talent and we were all saddened by his passing. He told me he would never have made it as a racer at Indian had it not been for your help. You were an inspiration to him. We at Excelsior would be glad to have you on our team. As you probably know, our big valve racers are unbeatable, but we must keep our noses to the grindstone to keep ahead of the competition. I hope you can work with us in the development department, not only on the racers, but also on our regular machines, because that is where we make our money. Welcome, Fireball! How did you get that name, by the way?" Jed decided to prevaricate the truth, and told a modified story, just as Jake had when telling Schwinn about Jed.

Jed found working with Excelsior to his liking, and soon found himself helping with the development of the new three-speed models, equipped with electric lighting, which were to be introduced the following year. The major American manufacturers would offer these amenities for 1915, but Indian's electric starter would be forgotten and would not become a standard item on motorcycles for another half century. The war in Europe brought the large scale of Motordrome events to a trickle, as the factories geared up to provide machines for the Allied forces overseas. Jed found his activities at Excelsior taken up more with regular rather than racing machines. Nevertheless he did get to the odd race, and made it out west a few times to keep in touch with his friends, including Lucy Meredith. He managed to celebrate his 8th birthday at Lucy's pleasure palace on Feb 29th 1916 and, for the first time, it was all on the house.

One famous racing machine that was to become a legend appeared in this era: *The Cyclone,* produced by Andrew Strand at his small factory in Minneapolis. In the hands of their riders, Don Johns and D.O. Kinnie, these machines were unbeatable—when they managed to keep them running. The overhead cam arrangement took a fair bit of oil. While over-oiling fouled the spark plugs, under-oiling caused mechanical failure. This made it a delicate balance with the Cyclones.

"McNiel on a Cyclone"

Ignatz Schwinn, who had a fascination with the concept, told Jed one day, "We will build an overhead cam-racer one day, and when we do, we will get it right." When the United States entered the war in 1917, all industrial efforts went into war production; the development of racers was shelved until conflicts could be resolved.

CHAPTER SEVENTEEN

THE WORLD AND FIREBALL GO TO WAR

One of Jed's tavern visits in 1918, led to a break in his motorcycle career. He met up with long-distance racer, Allan Bedell, who had set a Henderson coast-to-coast record in 1917. As the evening wore on, Bedell's patriotism began to take an affect on Jed; before he knew what hit him, Jed had joined the army. As he was getting his medical the following morning, complete with a severe headache, the doctor examining said to him, "Your nickname is Fireball, eh? I can see why that is. They are a bit of a mess. Cough!"

Next came the issue of a uniform, then basic training. Shortly thereafter, he found himself once again aboard the Lusitania. This time there were no first class facilities, as even the first class dining room, where he and George had picked up the English ladies, had been converted to carry troops. It was wall-to-wall hammocks, a horrible transformation.

Jed's war was an easy one. Using his skills as a card shark and questionable methods, Jed's whole platoon was soon in debt to him—even the sergeant and lieutenant. This advantage allowed Jed to negotiate the easiest duties, avoiding situations anywhere he could get shot. His closest brush with death came after his platoon wiped out a machine gun nest at a winery. Jed had stayed well back during the shooting, but nearly drowned in a vat of burgundy after the fighting.

Because of his background, he was issued a motorcycle. He was assigned to DR duty well behind the lines. There was an instance when he made a wrong turn: his trusty J Harley took him, quite by accident, into German territory. Thinking he was liberating a French village, he waved at the German soldiers only to have them return the salute. The war was over. Jed's was one of the first Allied vehicles to enter Germany.

Our triumphant warrior returned home, after some great partying to celebrate the armistice, his footlocker was stuffed to the gunnels with cash in large denominations. He had visions of retirement as a permanent resident of Lucy's establishment. Unfortunately nearly all the cash was worthless, having been issued by governments and countries no longer in existence. For Jed, it was back to work at Excelsior. All at the company were impressed with the chest full of medals he had, not realizing that nearly all of them had been awarded to other soldiers who used them to pay off gambling debts.

Allan Bedell, a braver and better man than Jed, was not so fortunate. He died from the Spanish Flu Epidemic of 1918 that claimed more American lives than did the war.

Chapter Eighteen

Henderson Comes to Chicago
The Development of the OHC Ex

In 1918 Excelsior effected purchase arrangements of the Detroit-based Henderson Motorcycle Company. Jed became very fond of William Henderson, who had come along as part of the deal, and, especially, his wonderful four-cylinder bikes. Jed soon replaced the Excelsior twin he had been riding as a personal machine with one of the Henderson fours. The Henderson was light and lively as well as the smoothest machine Jed had ever ridden. He helped with some promotions involving the Henderson. This included supporting Blick Wolter in a clever publicity stunt when he rode around a roller coaster trestle at an amusement park in Southern California. Such stunts were the order of the day. Wolter was photographed with a smile on his face: 60 feet in the air on the top of the coaster. The Henderson climbed the slope effortlessly. This trip afforded Jed another opportunity for a stay with Lucy. This time he had to pay, but got a discount and a few extras.

Another part time effort was dreamed up by Jed. Using a borrowed Henderson and sidecar, Jed showed up at local racetracks as a representative of the Moxie Beverage Company. His "horsemobile" consisted of the required white plaster horse mounted in the Henderson's sidecar. All went well until Jed was caught selling bathtub gin on the side to mix with the Moxie. Fortunately, the scandal was kept secret from Ignatz Schwinn, who would have been less than impressed.

Coast-to-coast runs became popular in at this time as well. It began with Erwin G, *Cannon Ball*, Baker's coast-to-coast ride on an Indian in 1914, followed by a three-flag run in 1916, also on an Indian. Baker rode a Neracar coast-to-coast. Riders such as Allan Bedell and Freddie Ludlow set records on Hendersons. Jed was present as a supporter during most of the events on Hendersons, changing tires, and preparing the machines, often traveling ahead by train.

"Moxie/Henderson Horsemobile"

In the fall of 1919, when Ignatz Schwinn began work in earnest on his overhead cam racer, Jed was an enthusiastic helper in the race department. The Cyclone Company had gone under, like so many other small manufacturers, but even as late as 1919, the odd Cyclone would appear, beating the newer machines. The overhead cam "Ex" resembled the Cyclone, but had more robust valve gear and huge, two-inch exhaust pipes. Like the Cyclone, it had bevel gear—driven cams and magneto, but boasted superior lubrication up top as well as a more efficient breathing system to keep the oil from fouling the spark plugs. It was a tall engine: the "big valve" racing chassis it housed required extra height to accommodate it. It was the most outrageous racing bike seen in the world at the time, and for many years to come.

"Joe Walter on the OHC Ex"

The Excelsior team took the new racers to California, where they would race at the Ascot Race Track. Bob Perry, Joe Walters, J.A McNeil, Wells Bennett and Bill Church headed west by train, along with a factory support staff, including Jed Fleming. En route, Jed became quite friendly with Bob Perry and managed to take some of the young racer's money from him at cards. Perry was unaware of Fireball's special, marked deck. He had learned a few card tricks while hanging around Lucy's establishment, honed them in the army, and pulled off his deceptions with considerable finesse. These skills helped him sustain some of his bad habits.

At the Ascot track, the new machines barked like nothing else heard there before. At opening day of the 1920 season, January 2nd, Bob Perry was traveling at a rate estimated at 95 mph—faster than any motorcycle had gone there before—when he skidded entering a turn. Perry slid for a good distance before going down. He was thrown clear of the machine, but skidded into a post, fracturing his skull. The unfortunate Perry was taken to hospital, but never regained consciousness. He had announced beforehand that he was going for a wide-open lap, a foolhardy risk on a dirt track and on such a powerful machine. The Excelsior team withdrew from the race out of respect for Perry, and again from the following one just two days later. This left Otto Walker of Harley Davidson to win with a speed of 77.20 mph. Jed was certain that had they continued, they would have bested the Harley, but it was not to be. A dejected Excelsior team returned to Chicago, where Schwinn, who treated Perry as a son, ordered the machines destroyed. Jed sneaked into the factory at night, and rescued an engine. He couldn't bear to see these fabulous bikes obliterated from the face of the earth. Although he was to keep it for the rest of his life, it would be of little use to him except as a doorstop: the engine was the one from Perry's machine.

Back in Chicago, Jed worked on the further development of the Henderson, which now carried the X emblem of the Excelsior factory, and had been redesigned with side valves rather than inlet over-exhaust. The new machine, although somewhat heavier, was very robust and resoundingly successful, setting new records in long distance races. This new Model K was replaced by the even better Deluxe in 1922. Wells Bennettt rode one for 24 hours straight on the Tacoma Board track, the last board track not long before it closed. On May 31 1922, Jed watched as Bennett circulated for hour after hour, stopping only for fuel and minor adjustments to himself and to the bike. The Henderson droned on all through the night. At the end of the 24 hours, Bennett had covered 1562.54 miles, at an average speed of 65.1 mph, a record that was to last for fifteen years. Jed reflected back on the difficulties of his cross continental trip a mere 15 years previously. Motorcycles had come a long way in that short time.

"Bennett at Tacoma"

Schwinn was a difficult man to work for. There was also the fact that Jed had become somewhat disenchanted with the race department after the scrapping of the overhead cam project and Ignatz's loss of interest in racing. Jed decided to try his luck with Bill Henderson, who had left Schwinn in 1919. Henderson had objected to the redesign of the four-cylinder bike without his input and, although it was a good decision, it wasn't his idea. The new Henderson had side valves, rather than intake over exhaust. Further it was somewhat heavier, a retrograde move as far as Bill Henderson was concerned. Henderson began another company in Chicago and designed a new motorcycle, which he named the Ace. It was to be lighter and more nimble than the Henderson, and was destined to be the most glamorous of the American fours. Fireball was soon working for the Ace Company.

Chapter Nineteen

The World's Fastest Motorcycle

The Ace factory was conveniently close to Jed's home. He found that working there was much more relaxed compared to the Ex plant. Nevertheless cash flow was a bit tight, and on occasion they had to wait a day or two extra for their wages. Bill Henderson was such a good guy that no one seemed to mind these minor inconveniences; when he was flush their patience was rewarded with the odd bonus.

It was a sad day then, on December 19th 1922, when William Henderson was hit by a car and killed as a result of a fractured skull, while out test riding a 1923 Model. Would the company survive the loss?

The shareholders quickly secured the services of Arthur Lemon, an engineer who had worked with Henderson on his original machines and had moved on to Excelsior. Lemon realized that, for the Ace Company, survival meant it had to prove it had the best performing four-cylinder motorcycle in the field. He gave Jed the opportunity to work closely with him on some very special machines. To develop the engines for these bikes, the company invested in a dynamometer. Fireball became the operator of the $7500.00 machine.

The Ace Company worked on achieving as many endurance runs as possible. The dynamometer was not an important tool for the engines in the endurance machines, but meticulous assembly was, as mechanical failure was to be avoided at all costs. The test equipment was essential for speed record attempts though. For this the race department set upon creating a special engine. A new faster engine, known as the "Rochester" motor, named after a hill climb in that city, became the subject of some modification. To make it as light as possible, Jed, under Lemmon's direction, drilled the con rods, piston skirts and timing gears for lightness. He polished all internal parts, modified the oil pump and sump. Then he fitted the bike with a smooth, short large-bore straight pipe. Jed also installed an especially contoured, internally polished unique intake manifold.

The Ace Company called upon Maldwin Jones, ex Flying Merkel star, who worked for the Schebler Carburetor Company: they ordered an all-aluminum racing carburetor. Jed and Arthur Lemon together tuned the finished engine on the dynamometer. It recorded 45 HP at 5400 rpm. They then fitted the engine to an especially designed lightweight racing frame.

"Red Wolverton on the Ace"

On a cold gray morning, they took the machine to a straight stretch of concrete highway near Philadelphia. Here, under the watchful eyes of journalists, newspaper men, officials of the motorcycling world and Fireball Fleming, the Ace was finally ready for the test, Ridden by Red Wolverton, the motorcycle rolled through an electrically timed trap at the amazing speed of one hundred and twenty nine miles per hour. Wolverton repeated the performance in the other direction. Jed and a helper then fitted a specially built racing sidecar. With Everett Delong as passenger, Wolverton went through the same trap at an incredible speed of one-hundred and eight miles per hour.

The Phenomenal speed of the Ace, and the publicity surrounding it, served to stave off the threatened end to the company, but that day came in late 1924. Jed found himself without a job. There were plans to refinance, sell, etc., but Jed had had enough. It was a big disappointment after the excitement over Wolverton's successful test run; Jed decided he needed to do something on his own. He had been developing an idea. It was time to contact his Uncle George, who he hadn't seen or heard from in a long time. He needed financing.

CHAPTER TWENTY

FIREBALL FLEMING'S WALL OF DEATH

As luck would have it, good old Uncle George was all ears in hearing Jed's ambitious plans and agreed to help finance the venture. Jed's idea grew from his recollection about the board track racing days—how the bikes could run level on a very steep surface by virtue of speed and centrifugal force. The earlier, smaller tracks were usually steeper. If a track were to be constructed small enough, there should be no reason the bikes wouldn't stick to a vertical wall. If the rider could do some clever tricks while doing so, it could be a crowd pleaser and draw paying customers. He had, after all, become very proficient at riding while standing on his head looking backwards on that old Indian single a few years back.

Jed had liberated a new Ace from the ashes of the Ace Company, complete with sidecar and the exceptional Rochester engine tuned on the dynamometer that Jed worked on at the factory. After all they owed him some back wages, so it was a fair exchange as far as Jed was concerned. It was a bike that went out on test one day, but didn't quite make the trip back to the barn. With his new venture taking shape in his mind, Jed loaded all his worldly effects in the sidecar and headed westward—following much the same route he had taken back in 1907. He not only made the entire trip without having to resort to using the railway tracks, but, without really trying, almost tied Cannon Ball Baker's 11-day ride across the western plains on the Indian in 1914. Admittedly Fireball was no Cannon Ball Baker, nevertheless this feat underlined the degree to which motorcycles, and the roads they traveled on, had improved in such a short time. All he did, apart from minor adjustments to the Ace, was add fuel and oil. He traveled in luxurious comfort.

During the winter of 1924-5, with Derkum's help and Uncle George's money, Jed would see his dream become a proud reality. "Fireball Fleming's Wall of Death," as he called it, began to take shape. Derkum was more or less retired, but took an interest in the Wall of Death. Jed had decided to construct the Wall of Death in the Los Angeles Basin, where he had friends and where the weather was suitable for winter construction. He also reasoned that the season in the west would be longer for the carnival shows he hoped would find his daring venture of special interest. Best of all, he expected Lucy would admire him, as he would be in *show business*. He imagined the wonderful parties he would hold for his carnie pals at her pleasure palace.

Uncle George's financial commitment began with a half-dozen carloads of lumber and several kegs of nails. Uncle George arranged for the boys to use one of the railroad yards for the construction. Plans for the Wall allowed for construction in several sections. This would provide for ease of putting up the structure, then taking it down on demand. That is the sections would be portable to allow for travel with the carnival.

The Wall was circular, or rather like a standing cylinder in shape and open at the top. Overhead there was a cone-shaped canvas roof to protect spectators and performers from sun and rain. Customers climbed an outside spiral staircase to the viewing area. From the catwalk around the rim of the wooden drum, they could look down and watch the motorcycles traveling at great speed around the walls of the massive structure. There they were to see death-defying acts, featuring Fireball Fleming and, possibly, his beautiful lady assistants. Beautiful lady assistants? Well, this was an arrangement that Fireball had yet to firm up—to bring a pleasant dream-like wish to some form of reality. He had gone as far as to suggest to Lucy that she, and some of the girls, might like to make some extra money in a real show business venture. Lucy, however, was somewhat less than impressed. They were apparently doing well enough without having to go beyond the safe walls of Lucy's emporium. The only exception had taken place back in '22, after the death of William Henderson, when Jed was thinking he may need a new job.

He had become intrigued with a new design of motorcycle designed by Carl Neracher, and built in Syracuse NY. The little two stroke machine featured drag link steering, friction drive giving infinite gear ratios, full enclosure, and a center of gravity so low it almost steered itself. Jed took the train to Syracuse, along with Lucy and the girls, and hatched a scheme with Mr, Neracher to photograph "bathing beauties" on Neracars at a nearby beach. The photos were taken for publicity, but after straight laced Mr. Neracher was propositioned by one of the ladies, and he realized their true profession, Jed's scheme had collapsed.

"The girls on the Neracars"

The exterior of the Wall was painted in bright red to suggest that blood may possibly spill during the dangerous events inside. Gold lettering boldly traced the wording, *Wall of Death*. Further there was a rather flattering illustration of Fireball seated on an Indian—accompanied by scantily dressed ladies on each side of him.

"The Wall of Death"

Derkum was well connected in the carnival trade, which had gone hand-in-hand with the board track racing. He soon had Fireball's show up and ready to take to the road on the traveling carnival circuit. Fireball felt very much at home with the carnival people, as most of them were con men, hucksters, cheats, and card sharks, much like himself he had to admit.

The routine was that Carnival materials were loaded onto railroad flatcars for the journey to the next show site. Everyone pitched in with the repetitious tasks of setting up and tearing down. Fireball became quite accomplished in setting up the circus tent and loading the exotic animals in their cages. In turn, acrobats, freaks, con game operators and animal trainers helped set up the Wall.

By this time Jed had traded his prized Ace outfit for a pair of more practical Indian Scouts. He needed two in the event of breakdowns, and still had ambitions of training at least one attractive female performer. He rightly determined that the little 37cu. in. Scouts would be ideal for this work, given their low center of gravity, light weight, excellence in handling, and wide pan saddles, which were easy to stand on, either with feet or head.

The Wall of Death was usually set up next to the Freak Show. Jed became rather friendly with some of the freaks, particularly with the "Wild Man from Borneo," who was actually born to another freak at Coney Island. Then there was the Fat Lady, who was actually a man, and the Cave Man, a failed wrestler who wore leopard skin shorts and carried a Club with a stone spike. Cave Man resembled the comic book character, Alley Oop, and had only one heavy eyebrow. They were a friendly lot, but Fireball had met his match at the card table with this unusual crew. Wild Man, in particular, was a dangerous poker player; as his whole body, including his face, was covered with hair, providing the other players with no means judge his facial expressions.

Fireball, like the others, regularly took money from the "townies," especially in the Midwest. It was as easy as taking candies from babies. Although Fireball had a few furtive dalliances with women on the road, he was unsuccessful in talking any of them into running away with the carnival. His show was popular, but he felt it needed something extra, as a few other similar Walls of Death had appeared in other shows.

Occasionally, Jed would fill in at one of the other attractions between his shows. He often worked the popular milk bottle game. The suckers tried to knock down wooden "milk bottles" with baseballs. There was so much weight in the bottom of the bottles, that it was almost impossible to knock one over. Once in a while though, someone with an arm like a major-league pitcher would approach the booth. This is when the electro magnet, operated by a switch in Jed's pocket, came into play. The magnet could also be reversed, allowing the bottles to be easily tipped over on the rare occasions he allowed someone to win. This was to generate and keep up the crowd's interest.

"And the young lady wins a kewpie doll!" he would holler. Jed usually picked young ladies to win, hoping it would lead to some lechery.

Another popular carnival show was announced with the aid of a big bass drum. An exceptionally loud barker would holler, "Step right up and see Zorima, Queen of the Nudists, accompanied by all her nudie cuties!" Local farm boys would trip over one another to get in that tent—only to discover that Zorima and her entourage were not nude, but clothed in flesh-colored tights. This was not so much as a ruse, but an attempt to temper the wrath of the local constabulary patrolling the carnival.

Jed became a victim to such sly deceits himself: he took a fancy to Zorima, a tall statuesque brunette, until one evening he discovered that her sex was other than advertised.

One night, while drinking and playing cards with the lion trainer, Clyde Beatty, Beatty made a suggestion that got Fireball excited. Beatty owed Fireball a fair bit of money at the end of the evening, so settled up by giving Jed an old, toothless lion. "He still roars pretty good, Fireball, but he's harmless and friendly.

About the worst thing that could happen to you is having your face torn up when he licks you with his rough tongue. Look, I'll throw in a monkey as well, if you'll stake me to another hand. You can have the lion at the bottom of your wall, and tell the suckers it will eat you if you crash. The monkey can be trained to ride with you on the bike. You'll have the best show on the grounds!"

Jed built a cage for the lion. It was led out and allowed to enter the pit once Jed had motored up the wall. As if on cue, the lion would roar while the appreciative crowds would go wild with excitement. It was, as Clyde said, a real draw. He decided to work with the monkey, which created some problems. Fat Lady was enamored with the little creature feeding it licorice sticks, which the monkey devoured eagerly. Jed told Fat Lady to stop the treats, as it gave the monkey diarrhea. Jed wasn't so sure this monkey thing would work out.

One morning, Cave Man wondered over to the Wall, a mug of coffee in hand. Seeing Jed sitting on the steps with a glass of whiskey, he said with a grin, "A bit early for that, isn't it, Fireball? The suckers will be coming through the gates in another hour or so. I'd hate to see you fall off and get eaten by that ferocious lion."

"I ought to kill Fat Lady!" grumbled Jed. "I can't open today. There is monkey shit all over in there! What a God Damned mess!"

"What happened?" asked Cave Man.

"I was working with the monkey. I was at the bottom of the wall, sitting on the bike with the engine running, so the monkey could get used to the load sound. I had him doing handstands on the handlebars, and thought to myself, 'this might be good,' when the door opened and in walked the lion. I guess I forgot to latch the cage. As if on cue, the old bugger let off a roar and that monkey took off like a shot. He ran up and around that wall way faster than I have ever seen a motorcycle travel, shitting continuously. You should have seen that stuff spraying out of that blue ass of his! Everything inside is plastered! The monkey went over the top, and scrambled down the road in a cloud of dust. Good riddance!"

"Jesus!" said Cave Man, "What about the lion?"

"Oh, he just stretched, farted and ambled back into his cage like nothing had happened. He's almost blind, but you'd think he could smell that stuff. He's way less trouble than a bloody monkey."

With Cave Man's help, Jed dragged the fire pump to the Wall, and had the mess hosed down by opening time. "We have an expression here, Fireball," said Cave Man with a smile, "The Show must go on." And so it did, but without the monkey.

Jed stayed with the carnival act until 1929, the year the lion died of a heart attack while roaring at Jed one day. Jed was upset for weeks, as he had become rather fond of the old animal. He would have liked another, but Clyde Beatty had moved on to better things with his lion act. Jed was out of luck. He did finally pick up a female assistant though, so the lion was soon forgotten. Things were looking up in the Jed's world.

While the carnies read of the great stock market crash and speculated as to what it would bring to their world. They deduced that the economic upheaval would have no affect on them, as the suckers were still able to find a quarter or two to spend. For the carnival folk, life was normal, or so they believed.

Returning from a walk around a new town the carnival was playing one spring morning in 1930, Jed was alarmed to find a padlock on the entrance door to the Wall. A man in a bowler hat stood by motionless, until he handed Jed some papers. "Our bank is foreclosing on this fleabag outfit, Mr. Fleming. No payments have been made on your loan for several months. Your Boston investor is in default."

"What about my bikes, and other stuff?" said Jed.

"Tough ass, Mr. Fleming. I doubt the bank will get 10 cents on the dollar, so your other assets will have to be added in to help make up some of the difference, I'm afraid. We are all in deep shit. If the bank goes under, I'll lose my job as well."

Fortunately he still had the railroad pass his uncle had given him. Jed decided he had better travel to Boston to meet with Uncle George and to see what could be made of all of this. He looked at the Wall as if for the first time. A wad of burning bile rose to his mouth as he looked for a place to sit down. Jed was unsteady as he approached a bench by the entrance to the Wall, where his legs gave out as he lowered himself to the bench. A wave of nausea passed over Jed as he looked up at the painting of Fireball proudly seated on the Indian motorcycle. "Where is this all leading," he mumbled to no one in particular, "to nowhere good I suspect."

Chapter Twenty-One

Tacoma Washington, 1944

Jed Fleming's memories of his motorcycling life slipped from his mind as he felt the cold begin to penetrate the thin walls of his shack that had served as his home for a good long time. He needed to stoke the fire again. As he got up to do so, he was overcome with dizziness and realized he had a whopping headache. "To much damn booze last night," he thought, looking at the empty jug on the table. It seemed a bit odd, as he was seldom bothered by hangovers. Drinking alone was a bad habit, he had been told, but what could a guy do when there was no one to share the bottle with? As he threw in more wood from the Tacoma board track, he reflected upon the women in his life, a comforting pleasure for Jed.

He had had a pretty good thing going with a blonde waitress at the coffee shop until she ran away with that smart-assed salesman with the big Packard last month. What she saw in that asshole, he couldn't quite figure out. He had never had much luck with women, beginning with Mabel those many years ago. "I wonder where she is?" he said to himself, trying without luck to recall in his mind what she looked like. He also knew he and she had a son out there somewhere and wondered what he must look like. Like his old man?

The most significant woman in his life had been Lucy Meredith. "A hooker for Christ Sakes," he said aloud. He hadn't seen her since that day in the mid-thirties, the time he had gone once more to L.A., thinking he might find work there. No such bloody luck. He played their last meeting over in his mind, a nagging habit of his.

Jed had traveled to L.A. by train that time, but it was no first-class trip compliments of his rich Uncle George. Old George, poor bugger, had thrown himself out of his office window in Boston, shortly after the stock market crash of 1929. This time Jed rode in boxcars, not in a private car as he had done in 1907, when they traveled together to Ormond Beach. After being thrown off trains a few times, he had finally made it to the Los Angeles rail yards. After cleaning himself up somewhat, he set out by foot for Madame Meredith's so-called pleasure emporium. "Was it still there?" he wondered. With night approaching, he hoped she might put him up.

On arriving at the big house, which looked much the same but in need of a paint job, he knocked tentatively. "Is Madame Meredith in?" he asked the handsome black butler, who guarded the open door.

"Who is calling?" was the reply. The servant's suspicious expression was a good deal less than welcoming.

"Tell her that Fireball Fleming wishes an audience," Jed managed to get out.

After a few moments, Lucy appeared at the door. Still pretty, she had some telltale lines on her face—a face that did not hold the usual warm smile. "Go around back, Fireball. I can't have you traipsing through the house looking like that. We have some very high-class visitors tonight. Errol Flynn has dropped by with some pals. Eulah, the cook, will get you something to eat." With that, she abruptly closed the massive door.

"She always wanted to be in show business," mumbled Jed to the closed door. "Now show business is getting into her."

At the rear entrance, Eulah was ready for him. "Lordy, Lordy, is that you Mr. Fireball? You sure is lookin' a mess! Things have sure changed in this ol' world!"

Jed was soon tucking into a steak dinner, washing it down with a fine beer. Eulah said she had never seen anyone so hungry, and she was probably right. As he was finishing up, the door to the kitchen opened to an angry Lucy.

"You sure have gone downhill, Jed. You haven't shaved for days, obviously. Your clothes are disgusting, and you smell like an outhouse. After he's eaten his fill, Eulah, you'd better throw the bum out." With that, she turned on her heel, and with a rustle of silk, disappeared towards the front of the house. Jed was never to see her again.

"Hookers," Jed thought. "That's mostly what I ended up with. Lucy did seem a bit different, but in the end, they're all the same. That's probably all I deserved anyway. I've outlived some far better men."

He thought fondly of Eddy Hasha, Jake DeRosier and Bob Perry, all of whom he'd seen breathe their last so many years ago, and whom he had taken advantage of while they were alive. He settled back in his chair, nursing the nausea and headache, letting sleep carry him off.

There was no smoke curling from the crack in the top of the old stove. While the fire was burning well, what the troublesome crack emitted was an odorless, colorless, carbon monoxide gas. When it burned down—to dusty ash—the cold returned, a cold that Fireball Fleming was well beyond feeling.

ACKNOWLEDGEMENTS

I would like to thank those latter day scholars and authors who have sorted through the old photos, articles and stories, and have assembled much of the information I have used in this book, particularly Stephen Wright, Jerry Hatfield, Harry Sucher, Ted Hodgdon, Ed Youngblood, Herb Wagner, Herb Glass, George Yarocki, Frank Westfall, the Stanley Museum, and various other members of The Antique Motorcycle Club of America, past and present.

My editor, John Somerset deserves special kudos as well. The following letter appeared mysteriously on John's computer screen as he was wrapping up the text.

A Letter to the Editor, John Somerset, from the "other side"

Dec 20/06

Dear John:

I want to thank you for helping Gagan with my creation by cleaning up his lousy writing. It's a great job, and much appreciated.

Speaking of the creator, I was watching him on my new flat screen TV riding around that racetrack in England last summer. Christ, he rides like an old lady! What a bloody embarrassment. At least I understand why he made me a mediocre racer. Too bad he didn't make me a better person. I would have had an easier time getting in here if he had.

Things are pretty good up here. I got in with a fake ID. Uncle George, DeRosier, and all my other pals are here. Lucy (who lived to be 101) and the girls finally arrived, so I can have a poke whenever I want, and there's lots of booze. The lion's here, and we walk together each morning, where we usually see Sylvester Roper whizzing by on his steam cycle. No sign of the monkey, but that's OK by me. Pennington didn't make it either. I don't get hangovers any more, and that's good, because that last one I had down there before leaving was a real bitch!

You guys are both getting pretty old, so we'll see you up here before too long. I'll pour you one when you walk through the door.

Sincerely,

Fireball Fleming.

Last but not least, I would like to thank my wife Mary Jane, who has put up with my fifty year passion for old motorcycles for the last forty three.

Pete Gagan